Hope in the Storm

HOPE in the STORM

**GOD'S REMEDY
in the midst of the
GLOBAL FINANCIAL CRISIS**

UGO IKPEAZU

Copyright © 2011—Ugo Ikpeazu

All rights reserved. This book is protected under the copyright laws. This book may not be copied or reprinted for commercial gain or profit. The use of short quotations or occasional page copying for personal or group study is permitted and encouraged. Permission will be granted upon request. Unless otherwise identified, Scripture quotations are taken from the King James Version. Scripture quotations marked NIV are from the Holy Bible, New International Version®, Copyright © 1973, 1978, 1984 International Bible Society. Used by permission of Zondervan. All rights reserved. Scripture quotations marked NKJV are from the New King James Version. Copyright © 1982 by Thomas Nelson, Inc. Used by permission. All rights reserved. All emphasis within Scripture is the author's own.

Please note that Destiny Image Europe's publishing style capitalizes certain pronouns in Scripture that refer to the Father, Son, and Holy Spirit, and may differ from some Bible publishers' styles. Take note that the name satan and related names are not capitalized. We choose not to acknowledge him, even to the point of violating grammatical rules.

DESTINY IMAGE™ EUROPE srl
Via Maiella, 1
66020 San Giovanni Teatino (Ch) – Italy

"Changing the world, one book at a time."

This book and all other Destiny Image™ Europe books are available at Christian bookstores and distributors worldwide.

To order products, or for any other correspondence:

DESTINY IMAGE™ EUROPE srl
Via della Scafa 29/14
65013 Città Sant'Angelo (Pe) – Italy
Tel. +39 085 4716623 • +39 085 8670146
Fax: +39 085 9090113
Email: info@eurodestinyimage.com

Or reach us on the Internet: www.eurodestinyimage.com

ISBN 13: 978-88-96727-11-9
ISBN 13 Ebook 978-88-96727-39-3
For Worldwide Distribution, Printed in the U.S.A.
1 2 3 4 5 6 / 14 13 12 11

DEDICATION

To the millions who desire to find hope, strength, and stability through this period of world economic downturn.

To my God and Savior who has called me, entrusted me with a message to the world, and enabled me to be a blessing to my generation. I would be nothing without Your love.

ACKNOWLEDGMENTS

No man is an island, and every success and achievement in life is a result of the support of individuals who have sacrificially contributed in one way or another. Here are just a few who have made this work possible.

I am eternally grateful to my wife and friend, Akudo, who recognized the call of God upon my life and received the ministry committed to me even when there was no tangible or visible evidence. Without you, I would never have had the courage to step forward. I love you.

Special thanks also go to Ronke Babalola, who not only opened my eyes to the need for this timely message to be written and shared with the world but also spent countless hours editing the manuscript to ensure that this book retained its original message.

I am also grateful to Helen Lugada, who took this book through its second phase of editing and handled all my correspondences with Destiny Image Europe, ensuring that I never missed a deadline.

To Dr. Eric Lugada, who followed through the entire process, carefully printing out all of the materials and working closely with Helen to ensure that I got all the support I needed. Thank you.

Last but not least, I would like to specially thank the members and partners of the Triumphant Ministry International, whose unwavering love and support have become one of the propelling forces in my life. I appreciate you deeply.

Contents

	Foreword	11
Chapter 1	The World in Crisis	15
Chapter 2	Overcoming Anxiety and Worry	27
Chapter 3	This Is the Church's Finest Hour	39
Chapter 4	The Sixfold Target of Prophecy	53
Chapter 5	Why and How Is God Shaking the Nations?	73
Chapter 6	God's Bail-out Plan	89
Chapter 7	God's Bail-out Instruction One	95
Chapter 8	God's Bail-out Instruction Two	105
Chapter 9	Six Keys to Praying Effectually	117
Chapter 10	The Love Walk	135
Chapter 11	A Message to the World	145

Foreword

One thing I like about my friend Pastor Ugo is that he not only preaches the Gospel but lives it too. I have seen his walk bearing fruit in his life and the ministry in spite of the economic downturn.

This book brings to mind the story of Moses standing before the Red Sea. He told the children of Israel not to be afraid, and to stand still to see the salvation of the Lord. He added, "The Egyptians whom you see today you'll never see again." God makes the same promise in this book.

Hearing what God is saying and interpreting what He is doing in these trying times will bring strength and stability to anyone who reads this book. God has once again spoken to His children and revealed the steps that we should take to go through this crisis. *Hope in the Storm* points us in that direction.

Warren Hunter, apostolic revivalist
President of Sword Ministries International
and Apostolic Sword Network
Branson, Missouri

I
The World in Crisis

This book contains carefully outlined divine principles. I have tried to present them in the exact form that God gave them to me shortly before the onset of the global economic and financial crises. They are timeless principles that will guarantee financial freedom for God's people both in the midst of the crises and afterward.

∼

Almost everyone agrees that we are living in very trying times and the things that are beginning to happen have become a source of anxiety among the nations and people of the world.

The world economy is in crisis; a food crisis looms on the horizon. Nations, even the very great ones, are being shaken to their very foundations. All known economic remedies and principles are failing and crumbling before our very eyes. Political governments are slowly losing focus and relevance with their people. The global capital markets are in distress, threatening the life fortunes of uncountable families.

In the midst of all of this turmoil, however, God begins to call out to those who are called by His name not to be anxious—but to be at peace and to rejoice.

> *Do not be anxious about anything, but in everything, by prayer and petition, with thanksgiving, present your requests to God. And the peace of God, which transcends all understanding, will guard your hearts and your minds in Christ Jesus* (Philippians 4:6-7 NIV).

Why is God telling the Church of Christ not to be anxious? It is because we are entering into the finest hour of the Church—hallelujah! Our anxiety tends to stem from our ignorance of the source of storms—whether they are of God or the enemy. Many tend to remain anxious even when it is recognized that it is God working through the storm, if we are unsure of His purpose through all of it.

Our Father wills that we should be anxious for nothing; hence, He tells us that He will not do anything without first revealing it to His servants, the prophets.

> *When a trumpet sounds in a city, do not the people tremble? When disaster comes to a city, has not the Lord caused it? Surely the Sovereign Lord does nothing without revealing His plan to His servants the prophets* (Amos 3:6-7 NIV).

BE ANXIOUS FOR NOTHING

The Oxford Advanced Learner's Dictionary defines *anxiety* as the state of feeling nervous or worried that something bad is going to happen to you or around you.

It is expected that with the challenges poised around us by the current global economic crises, many would be anxious. However, God, in Philippians 4:6-7, reveals that it ought not to be so. His people are to be at peace even in the midst of turbulence.

Where Does Anxiety Come From?

If we are told by our heavenly Father not to be anxious, it clearly means that the worries we feel couldn't be coming from Him. In addition to receiving His very nature at the new birth—when we accepted Him as our personal Savior—He has made His abode in us. Anxiety is certainly not a part of God's nature, and because we have been made partakers of the *divine nature* in Christ, it is also not part of ours.

> *Whereby are given unto us exceeding great and precious promises; that by these ye might be partakers of the **divine nature**...* (2 Peter 1:4).

The enemy understands that faith and anxiety cannot possibly coexist. He knows that it is difficult to exercise faith while nervous and worried. It is him, therefore, who speaks worrisome words to us and builds fearful imaginations in our minds. He often causes God's children to see only the impossible side in every situation. All around the world people are troubled because they are not able to see the positive side of the crisis. Every person's challenge is a window of opportunity for another. If God's people will be discerning enough, then they will begin to see that the current global economic meltdown is actually a blessing in disguise.

Why Does God Tell Us Not to Be Anxious?

I remember a story my father told me many years ago. It was about a teenage boy who was going away from home to enter college. Shortly before departing, his father handed him a zippered case housing a new Bible. The father's instruction: he was never to be anxious, no matter what the situation was at school, even financial; rather, he was to simply open the Bible if conditions were to became adverse.

Why would his father leave such a charge for him never to be agitated even in the most difficult of financial challenges? It is because the father had already made a way of escape for him. Tucked between the pages of that Bible were crisp fifty dollar bills, enough to last him the whole term and even beyond. If a financial storm arose in school, the solution for him would be found not in looking at the storm or the desperation around him but in simply opening his Bible. You can imagine how relieved he would be to find that his father had already made provisions for him ahead of time.

In the same vein, if God says for us, His children, not to be anxious in spite of the uncertain global economic future, it is because our future in Him *is certain*. He knows that as long as we do not cooperate with our anxieties, the things we are worried about will never see the light of day.

Why Do We Get Anxious?

Let's examine a few reasons for agitation among people, especially in the wake of the prevailing global economic situation.

1. Ignorance of God's Will

I have come to realize that very often our concerns stem not from the fact that we face certain challenges, but primarily from not really knowing what God thinks about all of it. If we know God's will and position concerning an issue, it will certainly stabilize our hearts. We see how this principle played out through a situation in Mark 4:36-38:

> *And when they had sent away the multitude, they took Him even as He was in the ship…and there arose a great storm of wind…and He was in the hinder part of the ship,*

sleeping on a pillow: and they awake Him, and say unto Him Master, carest Thou not that we perish?

Were the disciples of our Lord Jesus Christ anxious? Yes they were. Was it primarily because there was a great storm? No, the phase *"Master, carest Thou not that we perish"* reveals the cause of their concern. They were not really sure whether the Lord cared about their safety or whether He was even aware of the challenge they had encountered, especially against the backdrop that He was sleeping through it. If they knew that He was very much aware of the storm and that through it they were to receive a new spiritual experience, they would have been at ease.

If many of God's children had the slightest knowledge of what He set out to do in their lives through the current global economic trial, they would rejoice exceedingly. This storm is not for your *sinking* but for your *singing*.

How to Overcome Anxiety

It is often said that knowledge is power, and this is rightly so. Knowing the *cause* of a challenge makes it easier to overcome. Having examined ignorance of God's will as one of the primary causes of anxiety, dealing with it becomes more straightforward. How can we do this? **Seek to know His will.**

*That ye might be filled with the knowledge of **His will** in all wisdom and spiritual understanding* (Colossians 1:9).

We should always seek to know God's will in all aspects of our living. This principle finds application in our health, finances, marriages, and our relationships. Once the will of God is known, it becomes easier to maintain peace and stability—even in the face of difficult and contrary circumstances.

I expect one important question running through your mind at this point may be: *How do I know God's will in a matter?*

Answer #1: By searching His Word.

God's Word has something to say concerning every aspect of our lives. His Word is Him (see John 1:1). God's Word is God Himself telling us exactly what His position is in every matter. The more His Word floods our souls, the easier it is for us to discern His will in every given circumstance. When we invest time in His Word, we will not labor needlessly or anxiously in the world.

Answer #2: By asking His will in prayer.

> *Thus saith the Lord, the Holy One of Israel, and his Maker, ask Me of things to come concerning My sons, and concerning the work of My hands, command ye Me* (Isaiah 45:11).

Let's look at another Scripture:

> *Ask, and it shall be given you; seek, and ye shall find; knock and it shall be opened unto you* (Matthew 7:7).

These Scriptures reveal God's commitment to respond to our prayers. In these times of economic uncertainties, His will can still be discerned by those who seek to know it. The time and effort spent in doing this is certainly not wasted but rather wisely invested. Once His divine will is apprehended, struggles, anxieties, and worries are terminated.

We can overcome anxiety by knowing His thoughts:

> *For I know the thoughts that I think toward you, saith the Lord, **thoughts of peace**, and not of evil, to give you an expected end* (Jeremiah 29:11).

One way to stay calm and focused in the midst of trials is to constantly remind yourself of God's wonderful thoughts toward you and His unfailing desire to give you a glorious end.

His thoughts for us are not based on how or what we think about ourselves, neither do they change with what we think about the circumstances around us. Whether we think highly or lowly of ourselves is entirely up to us. It doesn't change the way *He* thinks about us. His thoughts for us are constant and good. Even though we become limited when we fail to see ourselves and the challenges we encounter in line with the way He thinks about us, that does not in any way reflect a change in the way He thinks about us.

It is important to state here that God's thoughts for us are not based on how or what other people think about us. He will never think evil about His own. When He chastises us, it is because of His good thoughts for us.

Very often, we are anxious and worried because we are not truly sure of what His thinking about us is, especially when we go through the low times in our walk with Him. I am referring to those times when we are neither high in works nor spirituality.

It is interesting to note that the statement in Jeremiah 29:11 was a revelation from God to Israel through Jeremiah the prophet at the peak of their chastisement. In fact, it was given as they were being filed out in chains and fetters into Babylonian captivity. Imagine God telling them how wonderful His thoughts for them were as He led them as slaves into the land of their enemies.

With this understanding, God's people can stay in quiet assurance knowing that He is thinking of something good for them in these times of crises.

2. Looking at Life's Giants in Relation to Ourselves

The second reason to understand why we get anxious is how we look at the giants in our lives.

> *And the Lord spake unto Moses saying, send thou men, that they may search the land of Canaan, which I give unto the children of Israel; of every tribe of their fathers shall ye send a man, every one a ruler among them. And they told him, and said, we came unto the land whither thou sentest us, and surely it floweth with milk and honey; and this is the fruit of it. Nevertheless the people be strong that dwell in the land…And Caleb stilled the people before Moses, and said let us go up at once, and possess it; for we are well able to overcome it. But the men that went up with him said, we be not able to go up against the people; for they are stronger than we…And there we saw the giants, the sons of Anak, which come of the giants; and we were in our own sight as grasshoppers, and so we were in their sight* (Numbers 13:1-2,27-33).

Let's examine the following questions and answers in relation to how we see the giants in our lives:

1. Were there really giants in the land? Yes, there were.
2. Were they really men of great stature? Yes, they were.
3. Why were the spies anxious and worried? The reason is simple: they made the mistake of sizing up the giants in relation to themselves. And as long as they did so, they looked like grasshoppers before the giants. What did they expect?

The difference between Joshua and Caleb and the others, however, was that *they chose to see the giants in relation to God's almightiness* rather than themselves. This obviously made them look like bread before Him. Simply put, Joshua and Caleb got themselves out of the scene and brought God into it.

The problem we often have is that we are usually quick to put ourselves in the picture. By this I mean that more often than not, our immediate natural reaction to the challenges of life is to look at them in relation to ourselves—our strength and abilities. Every time we respond in this manner, we end up with anxieties. The concerns and worries we have regarding the global economic shaking stem from the fact that we have considered it and tried to find solutions in relation to our human wisdom and individual capacities rather than God's.

If we can step aside and learn to bring God on the scene, we will discover how insignificant and small those giants really are.

The Greater One on the Inside

*Ye are of God, little children, and **have overcome them**; because greater is He that is in you, than he that is in the world* (1 John 4:4).

*For whatsoever is born of God **overcometh** the world; and this is the victory that **overcometh** the world, even our faith* (1 John 5:4).

These Scriptures are not in any wise a promise for believers to overcome the elements of this world, rather they clearly affirm that they have already overcome, because of the greater one on the inside.

God in all of His wisdom, power, and glory lives in us. In fact, the Scriptures reveal that He is actually at home in us through His Spirit—the Holy Spirit (see Eph. 2:22).

2
OVERCOMING ANXIETY AND WORRY

What has He done for us? He has made us overcomers. That a believer is not aware of or conscious of this fact doesn't change it. What it means is that they may not be able to walk in the reality of what is already there. The current world economic crisis is rightly named because it is of the world and for the people of the world. He that is in us, however, is greater than the combined forces of all the elements of this world.

Two Types of People

Two groups of people exist: those who are of the world and those who are of God. Let's examine both.

1. They who are of the world.

> *They are of the world; therefore speak they of the world, and the world heareth them* (1 John 4:5).

> *And He said unto them, ye are...of this world; I am not of this world* (John 8:23).

These Scriptures reveal that there are people of this world. It refers to those who are not in a covenant relationship with God through the blood of Jesus Christ. For such, being of this world has two primary significances.

First, it means to be governed by the values and principles of this world.

Second and very importantly, it means to be limited by your world environment. In other words, whatever limits the world around you invariably places a limitation on you also. This explains why there is so much anxiety among many people worldwide. They have become limited by the financial crisis rocking the world around them.

For such people, the only transition from anxiety to certainty is Christ; He makes all the difference.

Lets' now examine the second group of people in this world.

2. They who are of God.

> *Ye are of God, little children, and have **overcome** them…* (1 John 4:4).

> *For everyone born of God **overcometh** the world…* (1 John 5:4).

Another phrase for being of God is to be born of God. John 1:12-13 tells us what it means to be born of God:

> *But as many as received Him, to them gave He power to become the sons of God, even to them that believe on His name. Which were **born…of God**.*

Those who are of God are those who are born of God; those who are born of God are the children of God and the children of God are those who not only believe on the name of Jesus Christ but have received Him into their hearts as Lord and Savior. Such people are said not to be of this world. They neither live by the principles and values of this world nor are they limited by their world environment except through ignorance and disobedience.

God lives on the inside of those who are born of Him and He is the One who puts them over the crises of life. What to do in times of crisis is to look inward to see how great the challenges may be in relation to the greater One inside of you.

It will amaze you to see how insignificant the troubles actually become when compared to His wisdom, power, and glory.

3. Failing to Commit Our Challenges to God in Prayer

Continuing our "Why Do We Get Anxious?" reasons from the previous chapter, when we don't pray about our life issues, we are bound to become anxious and worried when they become difficult and challenging. What happens when we don't pray about a situation is that we often don't know what to expect; so in every instance, we are filled with anxiety.

Have you ever left home and started your day without praying? You probably felt different throughout the day. You may have felt anxious—not knowing how the day's activities would turn out. If anything unusual happened around you, you were worried. The truth, however, is that God's love and plan for you concerning that day didn't change just because you failed to pray. But failing to pray left a vacuum in you that brought anxiety.

Praying Produces Peace

Be careful [anxious] for nothing, but in everything by prayer and supplication with thanksgiving, let your requests be made known unto God. And the peace of God, which passeth all understanding, shall keep your hearts and minds through Christ Jesus (Philippians 4:6-7).

One principle clearly stands out in this Scripture passage from Philippians. We should learn to commit all of our cares, no matter how minute they are, to God in prayer, because what people pray about, they are less likely to worry about.

Even in the face of turmoil, the fact that you have sincerely prayed concerning a matter assures you that God is aware of it. This in itself produces peace. We should also learn to have an attitude of thanksgiving, because thanking God in advance, even when difficulties persist, shifts the ball into His court. The result is inner peace and confidence.

4. Disobedience

Another reason we get anxious is disobedience. I believe that the root of all of humankind's anxiety is disobedience. Adam became anxious and worried when he disobeyed God, so much that he hid himself with Eve in the Garden (see Gen. 3:1-10).

Abraham suddenly became anxious about the safety of himself and his wife Sarah when, in disobedience to God, he started to travel south toward Egypt (see Gen. 12:7-13). The truth is that God's presence didn't depart from him and Sarah because he departed to go into Egypt; rather, he lost consciousness of God's presence around him as a result of disobedience. This was the source of his anxiety. Sometimes the fears and worries we have may be signaling the fact that we have gone away from the will of God concerning certain areas of our lives.

Isaiah the prophet makes the connection between sin, disobedience, fears, and anxieties, "The sinners in Zion are afraid; fearfulness hath surprised the hypocrites…" (Isa. 33:14).

What to do when one recognizes this is simply to *return* to the place of obedience. Very often we find it difficult to make that *U-turn* even when we know that we should—because we are afraid of starting afresh, especially when so much time and effort has been invested in pursuing the wrong path. The danger, however, remains: *the longer we stay on the wrong path, the farther we go from the right one.*

I love the way Isaiah puts it, "For thus saith the Lord God, the Holy One of Israel; in returning and rest shall ye be saved…" (Isa. 30:15).

5. Predetermining Timeframes for Divine Events

Predetermining timeframes for divine events is one of the most common sources of anxiety and worries among God's children today. Very often even when we say, "God let Your time prevail in such and such a situation," somewhere in the back of our minds, we have decided it has to happen within a certain time period that we have set ourselves. When these things don't happen within our set time, we easily slip into anxiety and worry.

This was the cause of Israel's anxiety. They had decided that God would definitely show up before the summer and winter periods were over. When it didn't happen within this predetermined time period, they became anxious (see Jer. 8:20).

One may say, but Elisha the prophet prophesied plenty in Samaria within a 24-hour timeframe. Yes, if you read Second Kings 7:1, you recognize that he said, "Hear ye the word of the Lord—thus saith the Lord." It was *God* who set the time period and inspired His servant to declare it.

Are there times or occasions when someone is inspired to believe and declare a timeframe for a certain divine occurrence? Of course; yes. But be sure you are inspired, otherwise you may be setting up yourself for anxiety and worry.

I have been inspired to believe God for certain things within certain specified periods of time. I have even been inspired to make certain declarations that are time bound. However, I try not to get into the habit of setting time boundaries for God, especially because David said in Psalm 31:15, "My times are in Thy hands."

The truth according to Mark 11:23-24 is that God promises to grant us every desire that is according to His will *and* for us to have whatsoever we say.

The truth also is that the phrase *"you shall have,"* which occurs in two verses, clearly shows that there is a time factor that only God determines. The word *shall* can imply now, tomorrow, next month, next year, or even many years to come.

This understanding helps us keep our minds open in dealing with God and also keeps anxiety away from us.

Let's examine how God dealt with this kind of anxiety and worry in Daniel's mind (see Dan. 9:1-2, 21-24). In verse 24 it says, "Seventy weeks are determined upon thy people…." By that statement God was saying to Daniel, the only way not to get into the anxiety and worry that comes from feeling that this situation is taking too long is to yield yourself to My own timing. I know what I am doing and I know when the process is complete. Hallelujah!

Very often, our anxieties and worries stem from the fact that we are either too slow or too fast for God. That's why He admonishes us in Matthew 11:29 to take His yoke upon us as a way of walking and living within His own preordained timing for our lives.

In John 11:5-6, our Lord Jesus was told that Lazarus, the one whom He loved, was sick. The Bible says that because He loved him, He tarried still and ensured he was dead four days before showing up. What on earth could be the relationship between the love of God and a seeming delay?

In this instance, it was simple. Traditional Jewish belief is that if a person dies, the spirit hovers around for three days looking for a possibility of re-entering the body. However, if nothing happens, the spirit departs at the end of three days foreclosing every chance of living. The delay of our Lord Jesus Christ for four days was, therefore, for Lazarus to have an unquestionable testimony of being raised from the dead. Very often, the delays we experience, and for which we become anxious, are actually demonstrations of God's love for us.

Delays could be:

1. To ensure we are ripe and mature for what we have asked.

2. For the world to clearly see and know from where our help has come.

3. To use our circumstance to confound wrong traditional beliefs and preconceived notions.

To avoid or overcome anxiety and worry, we need to learn how to discipline ourselves to yield to God's own time concerning the various aspects of our lives. Having done that which we are expected to do, we should learn to wait on Him.

*He has made all things beautiful in **His time*** (Ecclesiastes 3:11).

See also Habakkuk 2:1-3, and consider Job's attitude in Job 14:14.

6. Predetermining the Pattern or Course of Events

Again, very often we ask God to have His way in certain situations, but in the back of our minds we decide what course they should take. Sometimes this is informed by the way God dealt with someone we know or heard of; while at other times, it is simply our preconceived ideas of the best way the situation should work out. When things don't seem to go according to our predetermined pattern, we become anxious and worried.

In Isaiah 55:8-9, however, God tells us how frustrating it could be when we try to box Him into certain stereotyped courses of action. He has His ways in the whirlwind and so can bring about the same result in an uncountable ways. We are never to assume that He will definitely show up the exact way He did for someone else. If we do, we may become anxious and worry when He starts to do His thing His way.

When in Genesis 37 He told Joseph he would be ruler over his father's house, no one ever thought the outcome would come through jealousy from his loved ones, betrayal, slavery, and famine. But all of these were tools in the hand of God in fulfilling Joseph's destiny.

Psalm 105:16-19 says that God sent Joseph into Egypt *through jealousy from brothers, slavery, and famine.*

John 3:8 declares that the life of the Spirit-filled believer cannot be stereotyped—how much more the giver of the Holy Spirit Himself.

7. Relating With the Past Incorrectly

Sometimes we are anxious and concerned because somewhere in us is the feeling that we are being haunted by the past, even though we are in Christ. For many in the Body of Christ, the negative experiences of yesterday must be responsible for the challenges and difficulties of today as well as those expected in the near or distant future.

In this study, we shall briefly examine two categories of the past: our past personal wrongdoings and negative generational trends.

Our Past, Personal Wrongdoings

Very often I have had difficulties getting Christians to understand that neither the sins they committed before they came to Christ nor those committed as believers for which forgiveness has been asked for and received, can or should affect them now or in the future. The uncertainty with which many of us in the Body of Christ live through life is a reflection of our lack of comprehension of this spiritual truth.

> *Therefore if any man be in Christ, he is a new creature: old things are passed away* [dead and non-existing]; *behold all things are become new* (2 Corinthians 5:17).

There are believers who cannot imagine that they can experience the favor of God even in the midst of the current global economic meltdown because of the guilt of the lives they lived before they came to Christ. The fact remains that the very moment a person is born again, his or her past ceases to exist. In fact, God doesn't even remember it—and neither should you.

> *I, even I, am He that blotteth out thy transgressions for Mine own sake, and **will not remember thy sins*** (Isaiah 43:25).

This message of blotting out our previous sins contains certain divine instructions that may make the difference in the finances of God's people. The temptation may be to disqualify ourselves from what God is doing because we have disobeyed some of these principles in the past. That shouldn't be the attitude. What to do is repent and begin to apply them in our lives.

The second category of the past I would like to examine is negative generation trends.

Negative Generational Trends

Sometimes a believer observes certain negative generational family trends and becomes concerned about its possibility of catching up with them. Many have wrongly interpreted Exodus 20:1-6 to mean that God visits the iniquities of the fathers upon the children. That is not true.

Let's examine it closely:

> ...thou shalt not bow down thyself to them, nor serve them: for I the Lord thy God am a jealous God, visiting the iniquity of the fathers upon the children unto the third and fourth generation of them that hate Me... (Exodus 20:1-6).

The active words in this Scripture from Exodus are "of them that hate Me." What God is saying here is that the sins of the fathers can only affect the children if the children chose to hate Him like their fathers. However, if the children chose to serve God, they will completely be free from the sins of the fathers.

This same principle was reemphasized through Ezekiel the prophet (see Ezek. 18:1-3, 19-20). I am certain that no one in Christ hates God. We may make mistakes, but that doesn't translate into hatred for Him. In Him, we become the seed of Abraham (see Gal 3:29; 4:1) and the offspring of God. John 1:12-13 says that God has no negative trends and neither do His offspring.

Every child of God can and should expect to stand out financially even in the prevailing global economic downturn. Remember that you can go through it shouting for joy.

3

This Is the Church's Finest Hour

At The Triumphant Ministry, the church I pastor in Nigeria, we are not anxious about the looming world economic and food crisis because on the first day of January 2008, by the word of wisdom, God revealed the following to us:

1. That the entire world was about to experience a major trial and shaking.

2. That in the midst of the shaking those who are called by His name, know Him, and walk with Him shall be set apart and exalted—if they know how to respond to these times.

Let's examine some of the Scriptures given to us by God.

> *Since you have kept My command to endure patiently, I will also keep you from the hour of trial that is going to come upon the whole world to test those who live on the earth. I am coming soon. Hold on to what you have, so that no one will take your crown* (Revelation 3:10-11 NIV).

> *Arise, shine, for your light has come, and the glory of the Lord rises upon you. See, darkness covers the earth and thick darkness is over the peoples, but the Lord rises upon*

you and His glory appears over you. Nations will come to your light and kings to the brightness of your dawn. Lift up your eyes and look about you: All assemble and come to you; your sons come from afar, and your daughters are carried on the arm. Then you will look and be radiant, your heart will throb and swell with joy; the wealth on the seas will be brought to you, to you the riches of the nations will come (Isaiah 60:1-5 NIV).

The days of the blameless are known to the Lord, and their inheritance will endure forever. In times of disaster they will not wither; in days of famine they will enjoy plenty (Psalm 37:18-19 NIV).

Blessed is the man whom God corrects; so do not despise the discipline of the Almighty. For He wounds, but He also binds up; He injures, but His hands also heal. From six calamities He will rescue you; in seven no harm will befall you. In famine He will ransom you from death, and in battle from the stroke of the sword. You will be protected from the lash of the tongue; and need not fear when destruction comes. You will laugh at destruction and famine, and need not fear the beasts of the earth. For you will have a covenant with the stones of the field, and the wild animals will be at peace with you. You will know that your tent is secure; you will take stock of your property and find nothing missing. You will know that your children will be many, and your descendants like the grass of the earth (Job 5:17-25 NIV).

This is what the Lord Almighty says: "In a little while I will once more shake the heavens and the earth, the sea and the dry land. I will shake all nations, and the desired of all nations will come, and I will fill this house with glory," says the Lord Almighty. "The silver is Mine and the gold is Mine," declares the Lord Almighty. "The glory of this present house will be greater than the glory of the former house," says the Lord Almighty. "And in this place I will grant peace," declares the Lord Almighty (Haggai 2:6-9).

The Lord gave us this word and these Scriptures in the early hours of the first day of January 2008 about the hour of temptation that will come worldwide.

The Sixfold Targets of Prophecy

Scripture references of God's intention and commitment to reveal His plans to His servants abound. The question is then, how does God determine when to reveal future prophetic events to His servants? For example, He revealed Israel's captivity in the land of Egypt, their eventual deliverance from bondage, and their journey into the Promised Land—430 years before its fulfillment. (See Genesis 15:13-14 and Acts 7:6-7.)

The prophecy of the birth and the Messianic ministry of our Lord Jesus Christ was given about 28 generations before the time it was fulfilled (see Isa. 9:6-7).

The word of the Lord concerning the current global economic crises, why He is trying the nations of the earth, its purpose for the church, and what His people ought to do—came to me about four months before its unfolding. Why is He so determined to reveal the future to His people?

The reason is sixfold:

- That we may have light
- That our desires may agree with His
- That our thoughts may align with His will
- That we may begin to see what He sees

- That we may fight the good fight of faith
- That we might know what we ought to do

Let's now explore each of these.

THE SIXFOLD TARGET OF PROPHECY—THE POWER OF LIGHT

Several Hebrew words describe light. However, for the purpose of this timely message, we shall examine four of these.

The first is *shachar*, which means a dawning. The idea here is the disappearance of darkness just before the dawning of a new day. This is what a word of prophecy does. It brings to light wisdom, knowledge, and ideas that were previously hidden.

The second Hebrew word for light is *epiphauo*, which means to cause to appear. The picture here is of taking away ignorance and bringing one to a place of knowledge. Until a person receives a certain degree of insight into the wisdom of God, life remains a cycle of struggles.

Photizo, which is the third Hebrew word for light, means to enlighten, illuminate, or open one's eyes to something. The secret things we understand belong to God, while those that are revealed are for His children.

Hagar and Ishmael struggled with thirst and dryness until God opened Hagar's eyes to a well of water that had been there all the while (see Gen. 21:14-19).

Through the word of prophecy concerning the current financial crisis rocking the world, God is beginning to open the eyes of His people to the tremendous opportunities hidden in the midst of it. When light is received, God's people can say there is a lifting up when the world is experiencing a casting down.

The fourth word is *apokalypsin*, which means to uncover. A person is limited to the extent of his or her ignorance. Very often, therefore, God will send a word of prophecy and through it unveil possibilities that no one had seen.

In the Beginning

In the beginning God created the heavens and the earth....
And God said, "Let there be light," and there was Light
(Genesis 1:1-3 NIV).

Looking at these first Scriptures in Genesis, you will notice that it was only after God brought forth light that He commenced the creation of the heavenly bodies, the stars, the firmament, the plant kingdom, the animal kingdom and finally humankind. Why was it so?

First, without light, there can be no life. The latter is a consequence of the former.

Second, even if life is produced without light, it will certainly take light to sustain it. All of creation is sustained by light.

Jacob's prayer for Joseph presents a striking insight into the importance of light.

And of Joseph he said, blessed of the Lord be his land.
*...And for the precious fruits brought forth by the **sun***
and for the precious things put forth by the moon...
(Deuteronomy 33:13-15).

It is light that the sun and the moon represent and brings forth the precious things of this earth. Just as light must come for the precious things of the earth to come forth in the physical, so it is with the spiritual.

Without light, there can be no existence of life on planet Earth. Humankind needs both plants and animals. The animals themselves need the plants in order to live. Without light, however, there can be no plants.

Light affects the sea levels, marine life, and rainfall, which, of course, determines plant lives and ultimately provides life for humans and beasts.

Light Determines Seasons

And God said, Let there be lights in the firmament of the heaven…and let them be for signs, and for seasons… (Genesis 1:14).

Just as physical seasons change by the effect of light, so do spiritual seasons. Every time God wants to usher in a new season, whether in the life of an individual, a household, a church, or a nation, He sends light that could come in the form of a specific word, idea, or an instruction. Light is like the seed that Heaven sows in the soul of a believer in order to produce a desired harvest, "Light is sown for the righteous, and gladness for the upright in heart" (Ps. 97:11).

Light will distinguish the church from the rest of the world in these times of financial turmoil.

This book is light (in the form of divine wisdom and instructions) which God has sown for the church in order for her to bring forth a harvest of His purpose in the midst of the current global economic melt down.

Benefits of Light

1. Light Causes You to Arise. "Arise, shine; for thy *light* is come…" (Isa. 60:1).

    Complacency, indifference, and laziness are all results of ignorance. People are laid back to the extent that they can't see what God is doing and their place in it. A man or woman to whom the plan and purpose of God is revealed can't help but arise. His voice in the midst of the shaking is a wake-up call for His people to arise to their place of honor and dignity.

The reason for the shaking is so that your life can make a difference.

2. Light produces passion.

> *In the first year of Darius the son of Ahauerus, of the seed of the Medes...I Daniel understood by books, the number of the years where of the word of the Lord came to Jeremiah the prophet...And I set my face unto the Lord God, to seek by prayer and supplications, with fasting...* (Daniel 9:1-3).

The passion we see displayed by Daniel through seeking supplications and fasting wasn't always there. It came as a result of the insight he received through studying Jeremiah's account of the events that culminated into Israel's captivity in Babylon and God's calendar for their eventual return.

The essence of the message in the pages of this book is for us to have the light of revelation concerning who is behind the current global financial challenge, the purpose for the shaking and the place of the church in the midst of it. This understanding should make God's people passionate about fulfilling His purpose for this season.

Light Produces Voice

*To the law and to the testimony: **if they speak not** according to this word, it is because there is **no light in them*** (Isaiah 8:20).

One of the most significant spiritual principles for walking in the reality of God's blessings is the confession of our voices. God Himself lives by this principle. Romans 4:17 reveals that He *calls the things that be not as though they were.*

The reason why an entire generation, except Joshua and Caleb, perished in the wilderness was because of their wrong confessions. At every instance, they spoke that God had brought them to die in the wilderness. The result was that God gave them that which they confessed. Their problem was largely that of ignorance. They had no insight into the ways of God because they didn't desire it. If they did, they would have known that He creates the fruit of the lips (see Isa. 57:19). One Scripture that connects this principle to the times we live in today is found in Job 22:29, "When men are cast down, then thou *shalt say*, There is lifting up...."

Men and women are cast down because of the economic situation in the world today. However, God through His Word admonishes us never to confess what we see but what His Word says. What does His Word say concerning His children? It says that in the days of famine they shall enjoy plenty. It also says that they will laugh at famine and destruction.

Notice the phrase "shalt say" in the Scripture from Job. Why is it so? Why didn't God just say, when men are cast down there shall be a lifting up? The reason is simple. *We first have to **say** it before we can **see** it.* The more light we have in the Word of God, the more our confessions change.

Light Leads to Your Inheritance

> *Giving thanks unto the Father, which hath made us meet* [able] *to be partakers of the inheritance of the saints **in light*** (Colossians 1:12).

There are two aspects of our redemption. The legal aspect, which refers to all the wonderful blessings we have inherited in Christ Jesus, and the vital aspect of our redemption, which talks about how much of what we have been given is currently being manifested in our lives. For example, healing has been settled as a legal aspect of our redemptive right.

Let's examine this fact in First Peter 2:24:

> *Who His own self bare our sins in His own body on the tree, that we, being dead to sins, should live unto righteousness: by whose stripes ye were healed.*

The phrase "you *were* healed" in this Scripture reveals that healing has already been accomplished by the stripes that Jesus Christ received. God is not coming to heal us again. He has already done it. However, this is the legal aspect of our redemption. The *light* of this truth will have to flood a person's soul in order for the person to see it translate into perfect heath and well-being, which now constitutes the vital aspect of redemption.

The same principle applies to financial blessings and all the other blessings that we have inherited in Christ Jesus. Just in case you are not sure whether you have been blessed in Christ, you need to read Ephesians 1:3, "Blessed be the God and Father of our Lord Jesus Christ, who hath *blessed* us with all spiritual blessings in heavenly places in Christ."

Just in case you imagine that the blessings are beyond your reach, I would love to draw your attention to the fact that believers are also seated in heavenly places together with Christ (see Eph. 2:4-6). *We are right where the blessings are located.*

God's Word is settled forever; therefore, every time He sends a word, it is accomplished in the realm of the spirit. However, it will take the light of revelation and direction for one to experience its physical manifestation. For example, His promise for His children to laugh and be in financial abundance through this season of economic crisis and beyond has already been settled. However, it will take insight and revelation for a person to begin to walk in the reality of that truth.

Not only have we been given an inheritance in Christ, God has also endowed us with the *grace (divine ability)* to be able to partake of this inheritance. However, it takes walking in the light of the knowledge of God's Word to access and activate this grace.

> ***Grace and Truth,*** *"...but grace and truth came by Jesus Christ"* (John 1:17).

Grace and truth are two inseparable virtues. Every time you find one, you will find the other. When God sends truth, He also sends grace. The reason is simple—grace reveals truth. It takes grace to access and comprehend truth. The truth of God's Word has come forth: this is the finest hour for the church. With this truth has come grace.

The question then is *how do we activate this grace* in order for us to begin to experience financial lifting when the rest of the world says there is a casting down? It is by obedience to *God's bail-out instructions.* I have outlined these instructions in upcoming chapters.

Light Produces Change

Change often occurs when a problem meets with a solution. Many have not experienced certain desired change in their lives not because they do not know what their problems are but because they are ignorant of how and where to find the solutions.

The beauty of insight is that it not only reveals what the problem is but how it can be resolved. This is exactly what God has done through the pages of this book. In addition to giving us foreknowledge about the economic and financial plagues that have besieged the world today and how long it has been divinely programmed to last, He has also shown His covenant people how they can stand out and be shielded even in the midst of it all.

Change comes in the place of fellowship and intimacy with the Father. The greater the light of God's Word that we walk in, the deeper the level of intimacy with Him. John the beloved makes this connection:

> *But if we **walk in the light**, as He is in the light, we have fellowship one with another…* (1 John 1:7).

When your light comes, your height will change. Light produces sight and sight produces height. The light you receive will determine your flight. A person who finds light, will undoubtedly fight for the right, because light produces might; light terminates struggles, because struggle is a function of ignorance.

When light comes, your plight will change. Where there is no light, life will become tight. The light you have will determine how light your burden will be. When light comes, life will become bright. Darkness is a function of ignorance. When you become an embodiment of light no one can slight you. At the instance of light, fear and fright will disappear. When you are a carrier of light, you soon become the delight of others.

4
The Sixfold Target of Prophecy

The Sixfold Target of Prophecy— The Place of Desire

Each time God sends a prophetic word, one of His targets is to bring His desire in line with His divine will. This is exactly what His voice, as echoed in the lines of this book, has set out to accomplish in the midst of the prevailing global economic challenge. He has revealed His will to His covenant children so they can begin to desire what He desires for them.

Two cannot walk together except they are in agreement (see Amos 3:3). If we are ever going to experience the promised, abundant financial blessings in these times of famine, however, we will have to desire it.

What Is it About Our Desires?

Every aspect of our walk with God begins with a desire, "Through *desire* a man, having separated himself, seeketh and intermeddleth with all wisdom" (Prov. 18:1).

In the words of David, the man after God's own heart, "One thing have I *desired* of the Lord, that will I *seek* after…" (Ps. 27:4).

Seeking is a product of desire. What you seek after is a clear reflection of where your desire is. You cannot have what you haven't desired, neither can you rise beyond the limits of it. Very often, God's people have limited themselves and God because they have equated small desires with spirituality. We may sound and look very religious in our desire for less than God has given us but certainly not spiritual. Because He is committed to granting us the desires of our hearts, God will not take us outside the regions of our desires. If we desire what He has said, sooner or later we will begin to experience what He has said. Let's examine a few Scriptures that confirm this truth.

> *He will fulfill the **desire** of them that fear Him…* (Psalm 145:19).

> *…but the **desire** of the righteous shall be granted* (Proverbs 10:24).

These two Scriptures reveal God's commitment to deal with us on the basis of our desires. To make the connection between what we desire and what we end up with in life, let's take a lesson from the Bible.

Lazarus and the Rich Man

> *There was a certain rich man, which was clothed in purple and fine linen, and fared sumptuously every day: and there was a certain beggar named Lazarus, which was laid at his gate…**and desiring** to be fed with the crumbs which fell from the rich man's table…* (Luke 16:19-21).

What was Lazarus's desire? Crumbs.

What did he end up with in his life? Crumbs.

Was Lazarus a righteous man? Yes, at least he went to paradise at death.

Did God place a limitation upon him? Certainly not.

Why did he end up in life with crumbs? Because that was all he desired.

Each time I read this story in the Bible, I never cease to wonder how Lazarus got to this point in his mind. His view about what he deserved in life had become so affected that he couldn't see himself beyond eating crumbs from the rich man's table.

People may be going through difficult and trying times, but they must never allow that to form the basis for putting a value on themselves. The only way to truly determine your worth is to look at the price that God was willing to pay for your redemption. It cost Him His only begotten Son, Jesus Christ.

What could have formed Lazarus's desire for leftovers? I have often wondered whether it had to do with years of abuse, lack, failure, disappointment, and disillusionment. On the contrary, could it be that he had become like some in the Body of Christ today who have come to view poverty and lack as a measure of spirituality; even though the Bible, in First Corinthians 3:21-22, clearly affirms that all things including this world and all of its vast resources are ours?

In that state of mind, there was very little God could have done for Lazarus. God Himself was handicapped by his desire even though he was a child of Abraham, His friend. Lazarus presents a picture of many in the church world today. We seem satisfied with the fact that we are on our way to Heaven. That, however, is not the only reason God saved us. He saved us also for the purpose of restoring us to humankind's original mandate, which is to be His under-rulers—ruling and reigning here on His behalf, irrespective of the changes in the economic, financial, and political environment in the world around us.

If your desire is just to get to Heaven, this message is not for you. It is for those whose desire is to live out their days as the days of Heaven on earth, "That your days may be…as the days of heaven upon the earth" (Deut. 11:21).

If your desire is simply to get back to Heaven, your desire is small, because in Christ we are already citizens of Heaven and ambassadors here. In fact, the Bible says in Ephesians 1:4 that God already chose us *in Christ* before the foundation of the world. What this means is that *we were in Him in Heaven* before we came down here.

It should sound strange that an ambassador sent from his country to another would make his major preoccupation to return to his native country rather than the advancement of his country's values, culture, policies, and interests. We are here to demonstrate Heaven on earth, and there is no better time to desire to do this than now that the economic systems of this world have failed. Now is the time for the church to show the world that Kingdom economics never fail.

The Birthing of Desire

Desire is birthed in the place of knowledge. What you desire will depend on the information you have. The information contained in this book is meant to ignite a desire in you to walk in plenty even in the midst of global lack.

Desire, when ignited, produces thoughts, and thoughts, vision. Vision produces faith, and faith, action. Action produces manifestation.

Knowledge is a function of what you hear and see. Therefore, people's desires are defined by what they hear and see. One of the reasons why many people's desires are limited is because they have not been shown anything bigger than what they have lived with for years.

When God's people become short-sighted in their desires, it is because they have not been told that they are called to affect generations. When we become conscious of the fact that countless destinies are tied to the choices we make, it will begin to restructure the content of our desires.

THE SIXFOLD TARGET OF PROPHECY—CHANGE YOUR THINKING

The third part of humanity that every word of prophecy seeks to address is our *thought pattern*. God knows that what a person ends up with in life is largely the result of the way they had been conditioned to think. Many of us have limited ourselves and God in our lives by the way we think. Very often, therefore, God will send us a word of prophecy so that we can begin to think in line with what He is about to bring into manifestation. It is only when we start to agree with Him in our thoughts that change occurs.

It is difficult—if not impossible—to experience God beyond what we think of Him. Little thoughts produce little lives, while outstanding thoughts produce outstanding lives. When a person's thoughts become dominated by failure, impossibilities, the devil, and all of his works rather than success, possibilities, and God's love and goodness, it will ultimately show up in the way he or she thinks and lives. Therefore, even when He has big plans for us, He can't bring them to pass because we disagree with Him in our thinking. Amos 3:3 reveals that two cannot possibly walk together except they are in agreement—this means walking with God too.

Know the Impact of Your Thoughts Before God

*Now to Him that is able to do exceeding abundantly above all that we ask or **think**, according to the power that worketh in us* (Ephesians 3:20).

Our God is the God of principles; and based on His principles as revealed in His Word that we have just read, He responds not only to our prayers but to our thoughts also.

The thoughts of the righteous have the same weight and impact as their prayers before God. The phrase "according to the power at work in us" indicates that not only is God's power at work in His covenant children, but that this power also responds to their thoughts and brings them into manifestation. This book is God's message to the church for this hour. It is a message of hope in the midst of global despair and of unprecedented financial increase in the face of the world economic crisis. If we are going to experience the manifestation of this prophetic word, we must first begin by thinking in line with it. We can't think differently and expect to see its reality.

Why Change the Way We Think?

Thoughts are like seeds. Once sown, they produce a corresponding harvest in due season. We ultimately reap the harvest of our thoughts. Let's examine Proverbs 21:5 (NIV), "The plans [thoughts] of the diligent lead to profit…."

Why would the thoughts of the diligent always result in profit, or plenty? The reason is simple. This person understands the principle of sowing and reaping, seed time and harvest (see Gal. 6:7 and Gen. 8:22). Diligent people understand that they must define their thoughts on the basis of the harvest they desire. Diligent people know that in order to reap a harvest of plenty, they must learn to think in terms of profit and plenty, also. There is nothing spiritual about thinking small.

Adopt a Creation Mentality

Many Christians are content with the thoughts of keeping their jobs, sustaining their businesses, and not having their houses and cars repossessed. While this is fine, it does not fully agree with what God is saying concerning this season. He is talking about wealth creation in the midst of financial turmoil.

God's people must change their thoughts from keeping their jobs to creating new ones, from sustaining their businesses to breaking new frontiers, from not having their properties repossessed to buying up new ones.

This is His message for this hour. Let us begin to arise and agree with Him in our thoughts. Refuse to think otherwise. We must begin to allow His almightiness to dominate the way we think. How can we who are covenant children of the Almighty God put a limitation on Him and ourselves by choosing to think like children of mere mortals?

We ultimately become what we think about, "For as he thinketh in his heart so is he…" (Prov. 23:7).

As people think in their hearts, so are they. If we choose to think like the world, we will become limited by its economic, social, and political elements. We are ambassadors of another government: the government of God. When we start to think in line with the principles of *His* government, we shall sooner or later begin to rise above the prevailing world situation. Remember; there is a power at work in you, waiting to bring your thoughts into reality.

Censoring Your Thought Pattern

In view of what we now know, God's people can begin to appreciate why His message to the church, as contained in the pages of this book, doubles also as a clarion call for them to begin to think like Him, especially against the backdrop of the current global challenge. The question then is, How?

1. Think in Line With the Word

> *Casting down imaginations and every high thing that exalts itself against the knowledge of God, and bringing into captivity every thought to the obedience of Christ* (2 Corinthians 10:5).

In this Scripture from Second Corinthians, God admonishes us to take hold of our thoughts until they start to fall in line with His Word. Christ is the Word of God; therefore bringing our thoughts captive into the obedience of Christ simply means getting them to agree with God's Word.

We should not allow challenging circumstances around us to define the way we think. Christ, who is the Word of God, should form the basis of our thought life.

When circumstances begin to define the way we think, the result is that sooner or later, we will limit ourselves to our circumstances. To rise above our circumstances, we should learn to think beyond them.

2. Think on These Things

> *Finally, brethren, whatsoever things are true, whatsoever things are honest, whatsoever things are just, whatsoever things are pure, whatsoever things are lovely, whatsoever things are of good report; if there be any virtue, and if there be any praise, think on these things* (Philippians 4:8).

Beneath every challenge is something good, and one way to access that good part is to think right. A person's thought pattern can become so conditioned to think negatively that the person can't possibly see any good even when it stares him or her right in the face.

Why does God admonish us to concentrate our thoughts on the positive side? The reason is simple. Thoughts are like magnets. You ultimately attract what you think about.

Concealed underneath the current global financial challenge are tremendous opportunities for increase. It will, however, take a person whose thoughts are focused on God, not the crisis, to attract these opportunities.

Remember Peter's experience on the stormy sea of Galilee? As long as he had his attention on Jesus, he rode the storm. He only began to sink because he got distracted (see Matt. 14:28-30). This is exactly what the Lord is saying to the church. The economic and financial storms are raging, no doubt; but God's people can stay on top of the rough seas if they know how to shift their attention from it to Him and His will.

THE SIXFOLD TARGET OF PROPHECY— WHAT DO YOU SEE?

Another fundamental principle for experiencing the blessings of God in an outstanding dimension is to be able to *see what He sees*. When God sends a word of prophecy, it is so His people can, among other things, begin to come unto agreement with Him by seeing situations from His perspective—not theirs. Let's examine prophet Jeremiah's encounter with Him.

> *Moreover the word of the Lord came unto me, saying, Jeremiah What seest thou? And I said, I see a rod of an almond*

tree. Then said the Lord unto me, Thou hast well seen: for I will hasten My word to perform it. And the word of the Lord came unto me the second time, saying, What seest thou? And I said, I see a seething pot; and the face thereof is toward the north (Jeremiah 1:11-13).

Why do you think God was asking to know what the prophet saw? It was for two reasons: first it was a crucial moment in his life. The time of the question marked the interface between Jeremiah's call and his commission. His office as a prophet had just been revealed to him earlier in verses 4 and 5:

Then the word of the Lord came unto me saying, Before I formed thee in the belly I knew thee; and before thou camest forth out of the womb I sanctified thee, and I ordained thee a prophet unto the nations (Jeremiah 1:4-5).

Although he had received a prophetic call, Jeremiah had to wait for the specific word of commission; or, if you like, the green light. This is where a number of Christians miss it. They sense they have been called to a certain field or into a certain ministry office but do not wait for the appropriate time to step out. The result is often frustration and despair.

What was the prophet's green light? It is found in verse 17, "Thou therefore gird up thy loins, and *arise, and speak*...."

With the words *arise and speak*, Jeremiah was released into Israel as God's mouthpiece. However, that moment did not come until he passed a test, which of course was the second reason for the question, "What seest thou?" God wanted to be certain that the man He was raising to impact the destiny of the Jewish nation was in agreement with Him before sending him to the people. If he was to go for Him, then he must see like Him. God's Word conditions us to begin to see things with His eyes, not ours; and the more time we spend with Him, the more it happens.

In late December 2007, He gave me this message. He spoke about a seven-year period of severe famine for the world that will at the same time be a seven-year period of tremendous increase for the Church of Christ, beginning from 2008. The idea is so that His people—the Body of Christ—can begin to envision and imagine themselves in seven years of unprecedented financial blessings in the midst of this current global economic meltdown. The world sees despair, fear, and hopelessness ahead, but we see blessings—hallelujah.

How Does God See?

God sees through the eyes of purpose. Each time He looks at a mess, He focuses on the treasure He can bring out of it. That was why He looked at a man called Abram—one who had been written off by reason of old age—and said, *I see Abraham as a father of many nations*. He looked at Sarai—a woman barren and well-stricken in age—and said, *I see Sarah, the mother of multitudes* (see Gen. 17:1-6 and Rom. 4:17-20). God looked at an intimidated, fearful, and oppressed man called Gideon and said, *I see you as a mighty man of valor* (Judg. 6:1-12). Gideon's response showed that he hadn't learned to see as God saw him (see Judg. 6:13-15).

Abraham's Lesson

Having told him that he was now the father of many nations, God probably noticed that Abraham had difficulties seeing himself, Sarah, and the situation around him in the light of God's Word. How could he possibly be the father of nations when the doctors had said neither he nor Sarah could ever have children?

God did something that was meant to move him from seeing himself in relation to his current circumstances to seeing himself in the word he just received from Him. When we begin to learn to see ourselves in His Word, no matter what the challenges are, sooner or later everything about our lives will begin to manifest His glory. Let's examine the Book of beginnings, Genesis:

> *And He brought him [Abraham] forth abroad, and said, Look now toward heaven and tell the stars, if thou be able to number them: and He said unto him, so shall thy seed be. And he believed the Lord…* (Genesis 15:5-6).

When God brought forth Abraham to count the stars, He wasn't turning him into a stargazer; rather, He wanted to leave him with a vision of himself as the father of multitudes. The idea was that every time he was tempted to turn his focus on his body, which figuratively speaking was dead at the time, he would remember the stars—the way God saw him.

What Abraham saw was important to God because people will ultimately attract what they see. Because of this action, Abraham believed God—why? He began to see himself in the light of the word that came to him from God. This is exactly what we as Christians are required to do. We have been sent a word of laughter in the midst of destruction and desolation and increase in the face of lack. We should begin to see ourselves in the light of this *word*, not this *world*.

The Sixfold Target of Prophecy—That You May War a Good Warfare

The fifth aspect of humankind that God intends to influence when He sends a word of prophecy is our resolve to fight. Paul the apostle makes this connection in First Timothy:

> *This charge I commit unto thee, son Timothy, according to the prophecies which went before on thee, that thou by them mightest war a good warfare* (1 Timothy 1:18).

Timothy was expected to put up a fight in the face of contrary situations through the prophecies that he had received.

That God reveals what He is about to do to His people does not automatically translate into the fact that every one of them would partake of it. It is those who are willing to fight who will experience its manifestation. The reason is because every time a word of prophecy is released, satan and his cohorts stir up contrary evidence to make it look like God's word is either not true or not meant for us.

At such times, it is the word we have received that gives us the impetus to stand in the place of battle until we see its fulfillment. Without such words sent forth, a person soon becomes discouraged and doubtful. He sends a message of hope to His people in the midst of the global financial challenge so that they will no longer be intimidated by the things happening in the world around them but rather be motivated to wait until their change comes. Apparently aware of all the contrary reports that were being raised around Timothy, Paul knew that the only way to get him to maintain his resolve for change was to remind him of what God had said and to get him to stay his mind on it.

One of the greatest battles believers are constantly engaged in has to do with standing on the Word of God. Satan knows that once a person begins to do this, very soon they will start to shine as light in the midst of darkness.

When God sent a word of prophecy concerning Israel's deliverance from bondage in the land of Egypt and their ultimate possession of the Promised Land, He knew they would encounter the Amalekites, the harsh wilderness conditions, and, of course, the giants in the process.

His expectation however was for that word to stir up a fighting spirit within them: one that will not give up no matter what until they enter the Promised Land.

Unfortunately, in that generation, only Joshua and Caleb understood this truth. The rest missed out.

> *And the Lord spake unto Moses and unto Aaron saying, How long shall I bear with this evil congregation, which murmur against Me. Say unto them, As truly as I live, Saith the Lord, as ye have spoken in Mine ears, so will I do to you. Your carcases shall fall in this wilderness; and all that were numbered of you…from twenty years old and upward…. Doubtless ye shall not come into the land…save Caleb the son of Jephunneh, and Joshua the son of Nun* (Numbers 14:26-30).

THE SIXFOLD TARGET OF PROPHECY—THE COLLISION OF OBEDIENCE AND DIVINE WILL

An important aspect of walking in agreement with God, whether for a financial, material, or spiritual blessing, is walking in obedience to divine instructions. For every prophetic word concerning what He is about to do, there is always an instruction on how to partake of it.

Prophetic and Instructive

The information contained in this book is both *prophetic* and *instructive* in content. Prophetic in the sense that the pages, like the sons of Issachar, give us an understanding of spiritual times and seasons in relation to current global financial events. God's message throughout, for example, interprets the world economic crises, reveals why He is testing the nations and inhabitants of the earth, and what He has set out to accomplish in the church through all of it.

As mentioned previously, God's desire and commitment to reveal events to His people long or shortly before they begin to unfold can be clearly seen in Scripture. Let's examine a few of them.

> *Surely the Lord God will do nothing, but He revealeth His secret unto His servants the prophets* (Amos 3:7).

The word *surely* in this Scripture connotes a definite pattern. It is as if God is saying, "This is the way I have chosen it to be: I will not do a thing without first telling My servants about it. Whether they recognize and respond to it is an entirely different question altogether."

> *Behold I will do a new thing; now it shall spring forth:* **shall ye not know it?** (Isaiah 43:19)

The active words in this Scripture are, *shall ye not know it.* Here God again affirms that He will not do a new thing without getting His covenant people to know about it. The problem is not with whether He speaks to His people; rather it is with the fact that they are usually not very sensitive to hear Him. Every father delights in regular communion with his children and so it is with our heavenly Father. In fact, it is an aspect of His attributes that is innate in humankind. We got it from Him.

> *Thus saith the Lord, the Holy One of Israel and his Maker,* **ask Me of things to come** *concerning My sons* (Isaiah 45:11).

Here it is as if God is inviting us to be part of the revelation process. What I mean by this statement is that we can actually set the spiritual mechanism for knowing the future in motion by simply asking. It is as if God is saying, "You don't have to wait until I show you what is to come; you can actually ask Me for it."

Isn't this enough proof that He really is eager for us to know about future events before their occurrence? Let's consider one more Scripture.

> *But when He, the Spirit of truth, comes, He will guide you into all truth…and He will **tell you what is yet to come*** (John 16:13 NIV).

This Scripture is unique in the sense that God through it begins to reveal to us that one of the mandates of the third member of the Trinity—the Holy Spirit in the believer—is to show us things to come. Whether we know it or not, He is doing this job right within us.

Every new season is characterized by new directives and demands from our heavenly Father. Every new season also consists of two major components:

1. Fresh opportunities and challenges
2. Gains and loses

What a person gets out of a new season depends largely on what they do with the instruction. What makes this book instructive, therefore, is the fact that not only did God reveal the current global economic crisis before its commencement, He also gave vivid instructions on how it can and should indeed turn out to become the finest hour for His children.

It is not enough to know what God is about to do or is currently doing. Knowing what we should be doing is also vital. This was what stood the sons of Isaachar out from among the other tribes in Israel. It will cause any child of God to stand out in this seven-year period of world financial famine.

> *And of the children of Issachar, which were men that had understanding of the times, to know what Israel ought to do;*

the heads of them were two hundred; and all their brethren were at their commandment (1 Chronicles 12:32).

The sons of Issachar stood out for two reasons: First of all they had understanding of what the seasons meant in relation to what God was doing; and second, they knew what Israel ought to do in response to each season.

This in a nutshell is the message of this book: understanding the current global season and knowing what the church ought to do.

5
WHY AND HOW IS GOD SHAKING THE NATIONS?

As the year 2008 progressed and events began to unfold in the international media, I went to the Lord and asked "Lord, why are You doing this?" The Lord gave me three reasons that I then shared with the church.

He said that the shaking we are seeing all around the world will get stronger and stronger, and it will terrify and confound many because the nations of the earth will not know how long it will last. The Lord said the shaking is meant to do three things: usher in a great strategic wealth transfer; cause repentance among the nations; and unveil a one-world government.

1. The shaking will usher in a great strategic wealth transfer.

...My cities through prosperity, shall yet be spread aboard... (Zechariah 1:17).

A good man leaves an inheritance for his children's children, but sinner's wealth is stored for the righteous (Proverbs 13:22 NIV).

Then the angel who was speaking to me said, "Proclaim this word: This is what the Lord Almighty says: 'I am very

> *jealous for Jerusalem and Zion, but I am very angry with the nations that feel secure. I was only a little angry, but they added to the calamity.' Therefore, this is what the Lord says: 'I will return to Jerusalem with mercy, and there My house will be rebuilt. And the measuring line will be stretched out over Jerusalem,' declares the Lord Almighty. Proclaim further: This is what the Lord Almighty says: 'My towns will again overflow with prosperity, and the Lord will again comfort Zion and choose Jerusalem'"* (Zechariah 1:14-17).

> *This is what the Lord says: "The products of Egypt and the merchandise of Cush, and those tall Sabeans—they will come over to you and will be yours; they will trudge behind you, coming over to you in chains. They will bow down before you and plead with you, saying, 'Surely God is with you, and there is no other; there is no other god'"* (Isaiah 45:14).

Through this shaking, the Lord is going to transfer wealth from the hands of the heathen into the Church for the primary purpose of the last and final harvest that will culminate into the return of the Lord Jesus Christ. What the Lord is saying is that the Church must become harvest-oriented. This transfer of wealth has already begun. Testimonies are coming in from Christians even in our local churches who never made much money in their lives and are suddenly beginning to make millions in the midst of this crisis.

2. The shaking will cause repentance among the nations.

Through this shaking, the wisdom and technology of nations will fail until all recognize that they are helpless without God. This will bring about repentance and the fear of God.

> *My soul yearns for You in the night; in the morning my spirit longs for You. When Your judgments come upon the earth, the people of the world learn righteousness* (Isaiah 26:9).

Through the shaking and the peace that the world will notice in the Church, through the shaking and the difference God will make in the Church, God Himself will exalt the Church—and the nations of the earth will become attracted to and come into the Church.

> *In the last days the mountain of the Lord's temple will be established as chief among the mountains; it will be raised above the hills, and the nations will stream to it* (Isaiah 2:2 NIV).

Let's examine two previous Scriptures in this context. (See Isaiah 60:1-5 and Haggai 2:6-9.) In these Scriptures, God promises the following:

- There will be a worldwide shaking.
- Through the shaking, He will fill His Church with glory.

When we examine the word glory and the first time it was mentioned in Scripture, it was in connection with tremendous wealth:

> *And he heard the words of Laban's sons, saying, Jacob hath taken away all that was our father's; and of that which was our father's hath he gotten all this **glory*** (Genesis 31:1).

> *Now Jacob heard the words of Laban's sons, saying, "Jacob has taken away all that was our father's, and from what was our father's he has acquired all this **wealth*** (Genesis 31:1 NKJV).

*Be not thou afraid when one is made rich, when the **glory** of his house is increased* (Psalm 49:16).

*Do not be afraid when one becomes rich, when the **glory** of his house is increased* (Psalm 49:16 NKJV).

Therefore, I believe that Haggai 2:7 could be read like this: And I will shake all nations…and I will fill this house with tremendous wealth and riches….

Just as the sons of Isaachar, the Church must know how to be positioned.

Men of Issachar, who understood the times and knew what Israel should do—200 chiefs, with all their relatives under their command (1 Chronicles 12:32 NIV).

By filling His house (the Church of Christ) with glory, which, of course, is the tremendous wealth transfer, and by the peace the world will begin to recognize in the Church in the midst of the crisis, God will exalt the Church to the point where the nations will begin to flow in to see what makes His Church different.

The word that Isaiah the son of Amoz saw concerning Judah and Jerusalem. Now it shall come to pass in the latter days that the mountain of the Lord's house shall be established on the top of the mountains, and shall be exalted above the hills; and all nations shall flow to it.

Many people shall come and say, Come, and let us go up to the mountain of the Lord, to the house of the God of Jacob; He will teach us His ways, and we shall walk in His paths. For out of Zion shall go forth the law, and the word of the Lord from Jerusalem. He shall judge between the nations, and rebuke many people; they shall beat their swords into plowshares, and their spears into pruning hooks; nation shall not lift up sword against nation, neither shall they learn war anymore (Isaiah 2:1-4).

And many peoples and powerful nations will come to Jerusalem to seek the Lord Almighty and to entreat Him (Zechariah 8:22 NIV).

3. The shaking will unveil a one-world government.

This trial is part of the series of worldwide events that will mark the build-up toward the institution of a one-world government and ultimately culminate into the emergence of the antichrist world ruler. Although we understand that the coming of the antichrist world ruler may be a future event, we should know that bringing the world institutions under a central control, which must precede his coming, will not happen overnight.

Through the global economic crisis, resource control is going back to the hands of governments, which is very strange and contrary to all that most of the world has worked for over the years. Much of the world structure strived to get control into the hands of the people; but suddenly by one move from Heaven, we can see governments buying back the control through various bailout arrangements. We can see governments buying major business. This is just the beginning.

How Is God Testing the Nations?

God is testing the nations by making the various institutions that have run the world gradually lose relevance. It appears that what those in the free world have labored for—control of the world resources to be in the hands of the people and not in the governments' hands—is being reversed by just one move of God. Governments are now buying up multinationals and the biggest banks in the world.

By returning control of the world's resources into the hands of governments, the gradual build-up toward centralized world control has begun. It may take awhile, but this shaking is the beginning. The world is likely to see the emergence of a one-world airline, a one-world stock exchange system, a one-world distribution system, etc. All of this will happen to centralize the control of world resources and power in preparation for the coming of the antichrist ruler.

> *He will extend his power over many countries; Egypt will not escape. He will gain control of the treasures of gold and silver and all the riches of Egypt, with the Libyans and Nubians in submission* (Daniel 11:42-43 NIV).

We see from these two verses from Daniel that by the time the antichrist ruler emerges, the control of world resources will have been centralized. The good news, however, is that before this point, the final harvest and the rapture of the Church will have occurred. I have shared with the church my belief that one day soon we will begin to hear of a one world airline. All the airlines will come together and all of this will be to set the stage for the world control of resources that will usher in the reign of the antichrist world ruler.

Even though these things are future events, we must understand that things do not happen overnight. There is always a build-up. It might take five years, it might take a hundred years, but the truth is that control is returning to governments.

I was reading in the news recently that various economic regions are coming together and soliciting for a centralized control system. This is not strange. God's children must be very wise and discerning; I believe that that this whole reversal of control is orchestrated from Heaven to set the stage for a one-world ruler. We read in Daniel that when he comes, he will exercise control over the gold and the silver of the nations of the earth. This is beginning, and it will culminate into the things we are talking about.

I remember that while Kofi Annan was the United Nations Secretary General, he once made a profound statement on CNN. He said, "What the world needs more than anything else is a world ruler." I laughed because although the man probably did not know the implication of what he said, he was actually echoing prophecy. We must understand and agree that we live in the final days; when we begin to see these events, the Bible says we must be like the sons of Issachar who had understanding of the times and knew what Israel was supposed to do in each season.

Every time you see a prophetic vibration, every time you see a spiritual shaking, there is always something the children of God ought to do. Every time the heavens shake, every time the nations of the earth shake, there is always something the children of God need to do. Once we recognize what we ought to do, there is always the need for a prompt response. We should not forget, however, that the solution we desire may not come as quickly as we may expect.

WE NEED TO BE PATIENT

For ye have need of patience, that, after ye have done the will of God, ye might receive the promise (Hebrews 10:36).

There are three prominent features in this Scripture from Hebrews that constitute the fundamental principles underlying our walk with God.

First, the will of God concerning any given situation has to be accurately discerned and obeyed. Having known and done His will, there is always a need to patiently stay through the waiting period.

This is the *second* principle and the one we will be exploring in this chapter. *Third*, the one who waits ultimately receives the promise.

Why Is Patience Indispensable?

I have taken some time to discuss this virtue in this chapter especially against the backdrop of the prevailing global financial crises so that God's people do not get caught up in the frustration that comes with ignorance of its place in our Kingdom walk.

Every aspect of God's Kingdom is driven by the concept of *seed time* and *harvest*. Let's examine a few Scriptures that establish this fact. The first one is a statement made by God in response to Noah's burnt offering shortly after the flood. It is found in Genesis 8:22:

> *While the earth remaineth,* **seedtime and harvest**...*shall not cease.*

The second Scripture is Ecclesiastes 3:1-2:

> *To every thing there is a season, and a time to every purpose under the heaven: A time to be born, and a time to die; a* **time to plant** [seedtime], *and* **a time to pluck up that which is planted** [harvest].

As crucial as the transition from seedtime to harvest is, this is the period when many sincere and good people of God lose it.

Ishmael—the Fruit of Impatience

> ...*And Sarai Abram's wife took Hagar her maid the Egyptian, after Abram had dwelt* **ten years** *in the land of Canaan, and gave her to her husband Abram to be his wife...And Hagar bare Abram a son: and Abram called his son's name, which Hagar bare, Ishmael...* (Genesis 16:3,16).

Having departed from Ur of the Chaldees in obedience to God (see Gen. 12), especially with the promise that he would become the father of many nations and having intimated his wife Sarah with the same word of promise, they both obviously had an expectation; and I can tell you that it wasn't in any way near the fact that they would have to wait for ten years.

We can therefore imagine how frustrated they, especially Sarah, would have been when they counted the years in anticipation. I can almost picture her saying to herself at the onset of the tenth year, *If nothing happens at the end of this year, I will have to do something myself.* The truth is that they both hadn't known God well enough to understand that patience is a fundamental aspect of walking with Him. It is for this same reason that folks sometimes become disillusioned in their Christian walk.

Abraham and his wife acted in their impatience and the result was Ishmael—the one who has troubled the entire world to date. Thank God that they both learned their lessons thereafter. How do we know this?

> *That ye be not slothful but followers of them who through faith and **patience** inherit the promises. For when God made promise to Abraham, because He could swear by no greater, He swear by Himself, saying, Surely blessing I will bless thee, and multiplying I will multiply thee. And so, after he [Abraham] had **patiently** endured, he obtained the promise* (Hebrews 6:12-15).

Abraham obviously learned the importance of waiting on God—a lesson we all need to learn. Managing the conflict between what we feel in our heads and what God is saying in our hearts is a challenge that many in the church world deal with. Very often, our heads want things to happen faster than our hearts—and God—want them to happen. The reason: one responds to our environment while the other responds to God. As believers, we should learn to listen to our hearts—that's where God is. He lives and walks in believers' hearts, which is their recreated human spirit, also referred to as the inner spirit, or man. Ephesians 3:16, Paul talks about God's *Spirit in the inner man.*

Patience in These Trying Times

It is possible to read through the pages of this book, know what God says about the economic and financial crises currently rocking the world, follow the clearly outlined bail-out instructions as given by Him—and imagine that things will change the next day. While this is possible, for with God all things are, it is important for us to understand that there is always a divine process for every prophetic manifestation. It may be short or long.

But a person may argue that Joseph went from the prison to the palace of Egypt within 24 hours. The truth, however, is that it took a 13-year processing period to get Joseph to his launching pad, which ironically turned out to be a prison cell. God can turn the most unusual and unconventional circumstances into a person's spring board for promotion. This is why Christians must begin to view the current global economic meltdown as one of their greatest opportunities for financial increase.

Wait for Your Harvest

In the parable of the sower, our Lord Jesus Christ makes the connection between patience and harvest. He affirms that for every seed sown, there is a harvest. However, some harvests take longer than others. We see this application even in nature. The fact that two different types of seed are sown into the ground, at the same time and under the same conditions, doesn't necessarily translate into the fact that they will both have the same time of harvest. One may take longer than the other. This is where the need to patiently wait comes in. Let's examine the parable of the sower.

> *But that [seed] on the good ground are they, which in an honest and good heart, having heard the word, keep it and bring forth fruit with patience* (Luke 8:15).

In this parable, our Lord Jesus emphasizes that a seed of obedience when sown often requires patience in order to reap its harvest. Every outstanding blessing requires a period of preparation, and this is what the waiting period represents. The longer it is, the greater the glory.

As we begin to apply the timeless principles in this book, it is important to emphasize that we may not automatically begin to see the financial miracles that God has promised in these times of global economic downturn. However, the fact remains that it will come; we just need to wait for it.

In the place of waiting, God begins to give us understanding of purpose. Many have a wrong understanding of the purpose for financial blessings, and in the words of Pastor Myles Monroe from his book, *Rediscovering the Kingdom,* "Where purpose is not known, abuse is inevitable." It is for this reason that God will sometimes take us through this experience so that by it, character is built in us. While faith can take a person to the top, it is integrity that will keep the person there.

A typical example of how abuse can set in if the purpose for a blessing from God is not known is found in Exodus 3.

> *And I will give this people favor in the sight of the Egyptians: and it shall come to pass, that, when ye go, ye shall not go empty. But every woman shall borrow of her neighbor and of her that sojourneth in her house, jewels of silver, and jewels of gold, and rainment: and ye shall put them upon your sons, and upon your daughters; and ye shall spoil*

the Egyptians (Exodus 3:21-22). (Read also Exodus 12:35-36.)

This event and its significance to current world happenings can only be better appreciated when examined against the backdrop of the fact that Egypt had just gone through the last of ten devastating plagues. Crops and livestock had been destroyed through a grievous murrain, hail, and a plague of locusts.

> *...And the Lord appointed a set time saying, Tomorrow the Lord shall do this thing in the land. And the Lord did that thing on the morrow, and all the cattle of Egypt died: but of the cattle of the children of Israel died not one* (Exodus 9:1-6).

> *And the Lord said unto Moses, Stretch forth thine hand toward heaven, that there may be hail in all the land of Egypt, upon man, and upon beast, and upon every herb of the field throughout the land of Egypt. And Moses stretched forth His rod toward heaven. ...So there was hail and fire mingled with the hail.... And the hail smote throughout all the land of Egypt all that was in the field, both man and beast: and the hail smote every herb of the field and brake every tree of the field. Only in the land of Goshen were he children of Israel were was there no hail* (Exodus 9:22-26).

> *And the Lord said unto Moses, Stretched out thine hand over the land of Egypt for the locusts, that they may come up upon the land of Egypt, and eat every herb of the land. ...And the locust went up over all the land of Egypt.... For they covered the face of the whole earth...and they did eat every herb of the land, and all the fruit of the trees...and there remained not any green thing in the trees, or in the herbs of the field...* (Exodus 10:12-15).

As a result of the plagues, Egypt had lost most of their food and cash crops; livestock had been destroyed, leaving the economy in crisis. The Nile, which was Egypt's main source of marine and aquatic trade, now stank by the reason of the dead fish, thereby crippling that aspect of her economy.

Egypt represents the world while Goshen is a picture of the Church. It is quite remarkable to note that in the midst of Egypt's economic distress, not only was Goshen spared, Egypt's wealth in terms of silver and gold was put in the hands of God's people. This was a strategic wealth transfer. What is happening in the world today is a reenactment of that event. The world is plagued by an economic crisis that is of an unprecedented magnitude. Stocks have been lost, businesses crippled, and governments are managing to secure the people's confidence. In the midst of it however, there is a Goshen where God's covenant people are not only spared and shielded from the plagues, but also positioned for the coming wealth transfer.

Just as the instruction then was for every Israelite to stay in Goshen in order to be shielded, so it is today. God has given bail-out instructions to the church, which, if followed, will result in tremendous financial increase.

Some of these bail-outs, however, come with patience; for during them character is built and purpose discovered. Because Israel did not fully understand the purpose for her financial empowerment in the midst of Egypt's economic plagues, she made a golden calf out of it and worshipped the creature rather than the Creator. The reason why some will have to wait is so that they can understand and align with God's purpose for blessing His children in these times of global financial meltdown.

6
God's Bail-out Plan

So we at the church began to say to the Lord, "Father, what would You have us do?" And the Lord said to me, "I have a bailout plan for My Church."

Every time there is judgment, there is also a blessing. We see from the Bible that every time God judges the ungodly, He blessed the godly. So the Lord has spoken. He says that in the midst of the crisis (not when the crisis is over), He will begin to elevate His Church. God will begin to elevate His people; God will begin to magnify His own, so that there will be a clear difference between those who serve God and those who do not serve Him.

Is this scriptural? Yes, it is.

> *And they shall be Mine, saith the Lord of hosts, in that day when I make up My jewels; and I will spare them, as a man spareth his own son that serveth him. Then shall ye return, and discern between the righteous and the wicked, between him that serveth God and him that serveth Him not* (Malachi 3:17-18).

These are the days when God is making up His jewels. These are the days when God is selecting His own. These are the days when God has come to place a mark of distinction between the Church and the world, but there is always something the Church must learn to do every time there is a movement in the Spirit.

What Will God Have Us Do?

As children of God, we understand that He makes a way where there seems to be no way. For example, He made a way for the people of Israel through the mighty Red Sea and caused Israel to walk on dry land in the midst of the waters.

We also understand that no matter how critical or hopeless a situation may seem, there is always good prepared for those who are willing and obedient. I mentioned earlier that each time we see a critical situation, there is good buried somewhere even in the midst of that situation. The good will only be revealed to those who are willing and obedient.

> *If you are willing and obedient, you shall eat the good of the land* (Isaiah 1:19 NKJV).

Hence, even in the midst of the global food and economic crisis, there is good buried in it for those who shall be willing and obedient to locate it. In the passage referred to in Isaiah 1, when we read verse 18, we realize that God was speaking at a time of national impoverishment. It was a time during which Israel was also experiencing a food and economic crisis. God told them that there was good even in the midst of it.

Just as we see the bad in the land today, there is also the good of the land hidden somewhere. It will, however, take people who are willing and obedient to the instructions of God to locate the good that is hidden in the secret places of the Most High.

So God is saying "Come, let us reason together." The enemy wants to make us believe that when we make mistakes we can find no help in God; but child of God, when you make a mistake you can *always* make peace with God. Go to your Father and say, "Lord, I'm sorry." He will abundantly pardon; and you, too, can locate the good hidden in the midst of the crisis.

When we are willing and obedient, then we shall eat the good of the land—even in the midst of evil and destruction in the land.

> *I will give you the treasures of darkness and* **hidden riches** *of secret places, that you may know that I, the Lord, who call you by your name, am the God of Israel* (Isaiah 45:3 NKJV).

God is speaking to us about these times—that no matter how bad the situation is, there is good somewhere. There is good somewhere for those who are willing to find it and those who will be obedient to the instructions that will lead them to the places where the good is hidden. In the passage from Isaiah 45, God says there are riches in secret places and there are treasures of darkness.

Remember also that what is happening to the world is what the Bible calls *darkness*, because one of the Scriptures that the Lord gave to me on the first of January was that darkness will cover the face of the earth and gross darkness will cover the people; but that upon the children of God (those who are willing and obedient), He would arise, and His glory will be seen upon them. So God says even in the midst of the darkness there are riches hidden in dark places—even in the midst of the economic crisis, there are treasures hidden in the secret places. That is what the Bible calls the *good of the land* even in the midst of the bad of the land, but it will take willingness and obedience to find it.

As we stand in our God-given places in the midst of this crisis, some of us might be instructed to change location. That is what it means when the Bible talks about the treasures of darkness. It speaks about the things our ordinary eyes cannot see. When the Bible talks about the riches of the secret places, it means some of us might receive new ideas. The Bible says the wisdom of God dwells with prudence and gives knowledge of witty inventions (see Prov. 8:12). God will give instructions that might seem stupid in the physical, but can take you into the place of power in the realm of the Spirit.

By examining various Scriptures in which God rescued His children in the midst of trouble, we will appreciate how His Church can stand out even in the midst of the current global crisis.

Just when it looked like all hope was gone, God made a way for His people Israel to cross over the mighty Red Sea.

> *God is our refuge and strength, an ever-present help in trouble. Therefore we will not fear, though the earth give way and the mountains fall into the heart of the sea, though its waters roar and foam and the mountains quake with their surging. Selah! There is a river whose streams make glad the city of God, the holy place where the Most High dwells. God is within her, she will not fall; God will help her at break of day* (Psalm 46:1-5 NIV).

We also understand that no matter how critical and hopeless the situation may seem, there is always good prepared for those who are willing and obedient (see Isa. 1:19). Therefore, even in the current world economic and food crisis, even as the entire global capital market is crashing and threatening the very existence of countless people, there are treasures hidden in the secret places of the earth, for those who are willing and obedient.

7
God's Bail-out Instruction One

Get Involved

God's first bail-out instruction is to get actively involved in the work of the gospel.

> *This is what the Lord Almighty says: "These people say, 'The time has not yet come for the Lord's house to be built'." Then the word of the Lord came through the prophet Haggai. "Is it a time for you yourselves to be living in your paneled houses, while this house remains a ruin?" Now this is what the Lord Almighty says: "Give careful thought to your ways. You have planted much, but have harvested little. You eat, but never have enough. You drink, but never have your fill. You put on clothes, but are not warm. You earn wages, only to put them in a purse with holes in it." This is what the Lord Almighty says: "Give careful thought to your ways. Go up into the mountains and bring down timber and build the house, so that I may take pleasure in it and be honored," says the Lord. "You expected much, but see, it turned out to be little. What you brought home, I blew away. Why?" declares the Lord Almighty. "Because of My house,*

which remains a ruin, while each of you is busy with his own house. Therefore, because of you the heavens have withheld their dew and the earth its crops. I called for a drought on the fields and the mountains, on the grain, the new wine, the oil and whatever the ground produces, on men and cattle, and on the labor of your hands"* (Haggai 1:2-11 NIV).

If you have been passively involved in the past and you want to walk in the reality of this prophecy, then get actively involved in the work of the gospel.

In the passage from Haggai, the Lord said that His house has been left to waste for which reason He called for a drought—such as the crisis we are experiencing now. But He also asked that the people consider their ways, repent, and get active in the work of the gospel.

This was God's exact bail-out instruction to the people of Israel in the time of economic hardship. They were to bear the pain and the inconvenience of embarking on the journey up the mountain to get wood for building the temple.

Why did God require that they endure the inconvenience of going up the mountain rather than letting them bring wood from any other place? This is because in the church, we tend to respond to the work of the gospel at our convenience. When it is convenient, we do it; when it is not convenient, we do not do it. However, there is nothing in the Scriptures that says the relationship we have with God is one of convenience. How would you feel if God only responds to you when it is convenient for Him? So God says: *You endure the trouble, inconvenience yourself, endure the pain, bear the burden, make the journey to the top of the mountain, for that is where I want you to go. I know there is wood everywhere, but I want you to make the journey to the mountain and then you will bring wood and build the temple.*

A sacrifice should cost us something. If there is no cost, it is not a sacrifice. It is called a sacrifice because you are giving up something in order to do it.

BECOME HARVEST-MINDED

For us today, the Church is not called on to build a physical temple, but to build lives. God is telling us to become harvest-oriented because the purpose of the global shaking is to usher in the great harvest of souls through the strategic wealth transfer. If harvest is the ultimate goal, then only those who align themselves with this goal will be positioned for the wealth transfer. If the purpose of the global shaking is to bring wealth transfer for the harvest, then the wise thing to do is to become harvest-oriented, this is how you position yourself for the wealth transfer.

The secret of supernatural provisions is to be aligned with the purpose of God. Walking in supernatural provisions is not just by praying, nor by fasting, but by aligning oneself with the divine purpose. Every provision is for a purpose, and if you can find a purpose with God, the provision for that purpose will naturally journey toward you. It is not God's will that the church should toil in night vigils for financial prosperity. It is not God's will that His children should run around to look for someone who will deliver them from the spirit of poverty. God's pattern has always been, "Align yourself with My purpose, and the wealth and the provision for the purpose will come to you."

This explains why the Lord Jesus Christ made a profound statement when He told us to "seek first the kingdom of God and His righteousness," and all the things the entire world is running after will run after you (see Matt 6:33). The secret of provision is purpose. The secret of power is purpose. The children of God should not pray for power. If you align your purpose with God's, the powers of Heaven assigned for His purpose will be made available to you.

This is, therefore, not the time to be a spectator in the scheme of events; this not a time to be indifferent to the work of the gospel. Make yourself useful to God in one way or another. Make a commitment that your time, your talent, your position, and the opportunities you have will be a blessing to the Church and the work of the gospel. Be fruitful; this bail-out instruction demands that you begin to approach God's work as if you are the only one who is left to carry on. We must approach the work of the gospel with this mentality.

GIVE GOD A REASON TO RESCUE YOU

Give God a reason to rescue you out of the global financial downturn. God needs a reason to rescue you, and if you are not going to be involved in the harvest, if you are not going to move from a self-centered mentality to Kingdom-centered thinking, then you are not giving God the reason to rescue you.

There is a story that is told of a man who was ill and at the point of death. He kept quoting the Scripture "I shall not die, but live to declare the works of God." God opened the man's eyes to see his service in God's Kingdom through God's eyes and it occurred to him that everything he had done was for himself. Then God said to him, "Can I find a reason to keep you alive?" It became clear to him that if God were to truly judge him, he had no reason to be alive. Thank God for His mercy, because this brother repented and was consequently healed instantly.

If you want God to rescue you, you need to act fast. For some people, their entire life savings are fast disappearing. What reason does God have to rescue you? Are you going to be involved in the harvest? Or do you want Him to rescue you so you can live life for yourself, so that life can continue to be about "me, myself, my money, my house, my car, my family"? Give God a reason to rescue you; get actively involved. This is not a season of entreaties.

On January 1, 2008, when God gave us this prophecy, some may have wondered what a pastor would know about the economy of the world. However, by the grace of the Almighty God, every word He sent forth from this ministry in 2008 has come to pass. I say this with all humility, because I know that it is not because I pray that much, neither do I fast more than the next man; it is simply because of His sovereign will.

So child of God, become passionate for the knowledge of His glory to fill the earth; be committed to the harvest of souls. If you cannot go, be prepared to support those who are ready to go. We have to truly begin to seek the establishment of God's Kingdom upon the earth; and when we become Kingdom-oriented, the world's losses will become our gain.

This is what God is doing through this shaking. Things do not happen by accident in the Kingdom. What you want should define what you do; define what you do to reflect what you want. When we become Kingdom-oriented—harvest-minded—the world's losses will become our gain.

Acquaint Now Thyself...

Acquaint now thyself with Him, and be at peace: thereby good shall come unto thee (Job 22:21).

For a long time, I had imagined that the word *acquaint,* in the context of the Scripture in Job 22, meant to know intimately. In other words, the more of God, His ways, and His will that we know, the more of the good things of life we will attract. This is definitely true.

In studying more deeply, however, the Lord led me to research the Hebrew meaning of acquaint and what I saw shocked me, especially when examined in relation to His purpose concerning the Church in the midst of the prevailing global financial downturn.

Sekan, which is the Hebrew word for acquaint in Job 22:21, actually has two meanings. The first one is *to be profitable*. If we replace the word *acquaint*, it will then read as, *Be profitable now to Him* and be at peace: thereby good shall come unto thee.

The second meaning of the Hebrew word *sekan* is to be useful. Again, the Scripture can be read as, *Be useful now to Him* and be at peace: thereby good shall come unto thee.

What God is saying here is that when we truly begin to be useful and profitable in His Kingdom, we will start to attract the good things of life, irrespective of the challenges around us.

The Divine Pattern

But seek ye first the Kingdom of God, and His righteousness; and all these things shall be added unto you (Matthew 6:31-33).

It has never been God's will for humankind to spend their lives pursuing the good things of this life. We were created to pursue the will of our Creator. The divine pattern is that as we go after the will of God, the good of this life starts to come after us. This may take a while, but it is meant to be so: unfortunately we have reversed this order in the church world.

The reason why most of our needs are not as fully met as they should be is primarily because we spend so much time focusing on them rather than *what God needs*. The more attention we give to what *He* needs, the more ours are met. This principle is timeless: it finds application not only in these times of global economic and financial siege, but afterward.

Some may argue that they have recorded success even though they have lived for themselves. If you are one such person, I would advise that you do not look at your gains in isolation; otherwise, you will be carried away by a false sense of success. However, when you consider your gains in relation to the time, energy, and effort put into the success you have achieved, you will suddenly discover how little you have received in relation to all the toiling and working round the clock.

For some of us, the compromises we have had to sometimes make in order to record the level of gains we have currently were too costly—they almost cancel out whatever the benefits are. With God, riches do not come by toiling or exertion; no, wisdom is the principal thing.

> *Labor not to be **rich**: cease from thine own wisdom* (Proverbs 23:4).

Financial increase through hard work is the wisdom of the world and this is exactly what we have been asked to cease from according to the Scripture in Proverbs 23. God's covenant children are expected to work hard but not to live by hard work. There is a difference between working hard and hard work. While the former involves engaging and exercising oneself in a productive process, the later is enslaving.

> *But thou shalt remember the Lord thy God: for it is He that giveth thee power to get **wealth** that He may establish His covenant which He swear unto thy fathers as it is this day* (Deuteronomy 8:18).

In God's Kingdom, wealth is a function of divine power; and this divine power, even though in every believer, is activated and appropriated according to the degree of their usefulness and profitability. In other words, even though divine power is an aspect of eternal life, which is the very life and substance of God that every believer receives at the new birth, its activation for wealth creation depends on a person's level of maturity and relevance in the Kingdom work. This principle will be examined in greater detail in an upcoming chapter.

The power for wealth creation is often manifested in the form of wisdom, ideas, and favor. God's wisdom will open a person's eyes to the tremendous opportunities that are concealed beneath a hopeless situation. One piece of an idea from Him can lift a person from the dunghill to a place of unprecedented wealth. His favor will open unimaginable doors. The more useful and profitable we are in the work of the gospel, the more access we have to these three dimensions of the *power to get wealth*.

8
God's Bail-out Instruction Two

Shield Your Investments

God's second bail-out instruction is to shield your investments from the global ill-wind that is blowing. We must understand that God's preferred method of judgment is usually to permit the attack of the enemy. The current global economic and food crisis is no different. By repeatedly permitting the enemies of Israel (the Assyrians) to invade in the times of Israel's disobedience, the Assyrians came to be known as the *rod of God's anger*.

> *Woe to the Assyrian,* **the rod of My anger,** *in whose hand is the club of My wrath! I send him against a godless nation, I dispatch him against a people who anger Me, to seize loot and snatch plunder, and to trample them down like mud in the streets* (Isaiah 10:5-6 NIV).

In all such instances, God always gave instruction that shielded and protected as many as were willing to obey His instructions. This was also the case when Israel experienced national impoverishment in the hands of the Midianites whom God had used to judge them (see Judg. 6:1-6).

There is a destroying wind blowing around the globe. Forget about the explanations that economists are giving. International experts in the field of economics, including a noted Nobel-prize winner, have thrown their hands up in despair and confusion, admitting that what is happening now defies all known economic principles.

Some have even been bold enough to say that we have to believe for some supernatural occurrence to solve the issues.

This is why we should take the instruction to shield our investments from the global attacking wind very seriously. These things are spiritual. The spiritual controls the physical. The current global economic crisis has partly been attributed to the pulling out of funds from the United States economy by Asian businessmen. The fact that China's economy is not spared in this crisis nullifies this excuse. There is always a reason, but we must understand that the things that are seen can be clearly understood and defined by the things that are not seen.

> *For since the creation of the world His invisible attributes are clearly seen, being understood by the things that are made, even His eternal power and Godhead, so that they are without excuse* (Romans 1:20 NKJV).

There are demon spirits at work, and God says you can shield your investments from their influence and the attacking wind.

God's Specific Investment Instructions

The following are God's *five specific* instructions for shielding your investments.

1. Obedience in tithes.

Those who are obedient to tithe 10 percent of their income should not to be tempted to begin to withhold because of challenges posed by the current global economic meltdown.

God says in order for your investments to be protected from the attacking wind, you have to be obedient in tithing. Please do not slow down. Since many have so much money invested in stock, or trapped elsewhere, the tendency is to begin to withhold tithes. God says, *Do not do it, because that is a lie of the enemy.* Where do you give your tithe? Where do you get spiritual nourishment? That is where you pay your tithe—the place from where you are taught the Word. This is exactly what the Lord has told me to say to His children.

You may say, "I have been faithful to tithe, but nothing is happening." Wait, there is always an appointed time. You should also change your language; speak God's mind concerning your investment. Confess that it is solid; it is shielded, that there shall be no loss. Why is it important to change your language? You can create what you want by what you say, even though it is not yet in existence, you can create it.

> *I create the fruit of the lips: Peace, peace to him who is far off and to him who is near, says the Lord, and I will heal him* (Isaiah 57:19 NKJV).

So you can create what you want to happen to your investment in stock, bonds, and shares by what you say. If you are obedient in your tithe but you utter negative confessions, you can cancel out your obedience through the power of your tongue. So you must match your action with your confessions, declare there shall be no loss; declare, "My investments are strong and solid!"

> *Beat your plowshares into swords and your pruning hooks into spears; let the weak say, "I am strong"* (Joel 3:10).

In other words, I can say my investment is strong. As you continue to say that, God will create the fruit of your lips, things around you will begin to reorganize themselves to align with what you say. It might take ten years, five years, five days, or five minutes;

but as you maintain your stand, things around you will begin to journey and align themselves around what you are saying.

When others are cast down, *we say* there is a lifting up. There shall be no loss. Let the weak say, "I am strong financially. My investments are solid"—such should be our confessions.

2. **For those who have been disobedient in tithing, God says: Repent and return to the place of obedience.**

> *"Go to Bethel and sin; go to Gilgal and sin yet more. Bring your sacrifices every morning, your tithes every three years. Burn leavened bread as a thank offering and brag about your freewill offerings—boast about them, you Israelites, for this is what you love to do," declares the Sovereign Lord* (Amos 4:4-5 NIV).

If you have not been paying your tithe, this is not the time to continue in disobedience. God says: *Return to the place of obedience, give your tithe where you are fed in the Word, give your tithe where you worship.*

> *"And I will rebuke the devourer for your sakes, so that he will not destroy the fruit of your ground, nor shall the vine fail to bear fruit for you in the field," says the Lord of hosts* (Malachi 3:11 NKJV).

There is a devourer ravaging the nations of the earth, and it is God who has permitted him. The only way God can rebuke him in your investments is when you are faithful in your tithe. Do you want God to rebuke the devourer and shield your investments? Then check your obedience.

If you have been faithful in your tithe, the Lord says He will make sure the devourer does not touch your investments. He says He will make sure the devourer has no access to them, through your obedience to your tithe. Things do not happen by accident. Whatever you see in the open is a result of what has happened in the secret places. Things are divinely orchestrated in the Kingdom.

3. Transfer your investments into a heavenly account.

Whether in stock, shares, or in bonds, you can transfer your investments from an earthly account into a heavenly one where they become untouchable. Every believer has an account in Heaven. Move your investments from your stockbrokers' account to a heavenly one. It might be physically with your stockbroker; but child of God, spiritually it could be in the heavenly account.

How do you do this?

> *Do not lay up for yourselves treasures on earth, where moth and rust destroy and where thieves break in and steal; but* **lay up for yourselves treasures in heaven,** *where neither moth nor rust destroys and where thieves do not break in and steal. For where your treasure is, there your heart will be also* (Matthew 6:19-21 NKJV).

The Bible advises that you should lay your treasure in Heaven, where the moth cannot destroy it, thieves cannot break in, and rust cannot mar it. Do you know why? These represent the global elements, the policies, the principles, and the conditions of the earth. Rust is of the earth, thieves are of the earth, the moth is of the earth; these adverse conditions do not exist in Heaven. So it stands to reason that when you move your investments, when you lay your treasures up in Heaven, none of the elements of this world can affect them.

> *Jesus answered, "If you want to be perfect, go, sell your possessions and give to the poor, and you will have treasure in heaven. Then come, follow Me"* (Matthew 19:21 NIV).

One way to lay up treasures in Heaven is to locate the poor around you, the needy around you, and reach out to them. Many of us are too selfish in the church; all we think about is ourselves. We do not care about the environment we live in, all we think about is ourselves and our own needs. No, enough of that!

You must find a way to reach out to someone in need. It does not matter how small, find a way to be a blessing for your own sake, because God says that is one sure way to move up your investments from your stockbrokers into your heavenly account. When you give to the poor and needy, you become a creditor to God. At times like this, while everyone else is in crisis, He starts to pay you back.

> *He who is kind to the poor lends to the Lord, and He will reward him for what he has done* (Proverbs 19:17 NIV).
>
> *A generous man will himself be blessed, for he shares his food with the poor* (Proverbs 22:9 NIV).

The second way to transfer your investment is by giving to those who minister God's Word to you. This is one profound way of transferring your investments from an earthly account to a heavenly one, where they become completely secure. If you have not been obedient in this, now is the time to begin.

> *Now you Philippians know also that in the beginning of the gospel, when I departed from Macedonia, no church shared with me concerning giving and receiving but you only. For even in Thessalonica **you sent aid** once and again for my necessities. Not that I seek the gift, but I seek **the fruit that abounds to your account*** (Philippians 4:15-17).

Learn to give to those who minister God's Word to you; you are not doing them a favor, but yourself. Some of them may not appear in need of your gifts; it does not matter. Paul admonished in the Scripture from Philippians 4 that his advice that the brethren give is not out of his need but that it may abound to their account in Heaven. So Paul said: My needs are met, but I do not want your account in Heaven to be empty, I want you to lay up your investment to your account in Heaven.

4. Shed every oppressive tendency.

> *Now listen, you rich people, weep and wail because of the misery that is coming upon you. Your wealth has rotted, and moths have eaten your clothes. Your gold and silver are corroded. Their corrosion will testify against you and eat your flesh like fire. You have hoarded wealth in the last days. Look! The wages you failed to pay the workmen who mowed your fields are crying out against you. The cries of the harvesters have reached the ears of the Lord Almighty. You have lived on earth in luxury and self-indulgence. You have fattened yourselves in the day of slaughter* (James 5:1-5).

Here we are instructed against using our positions of advantage to oppress people under us, whether in our office or business environments. We should not deprive people of what they should rightly have. Those who work for us should get their wages promptly.

5. Commit God to a harvest.

I recently listened to Oral Roberts' testimony of how during one of the great depressions in addition to securing his entire life investments in stock and shares, God gave him an astonishing harvest through the *seed faith* principle.

> *As long as the earth endures, seedtime and harvest, cold and heat, summer and winter, day and night will never cease* (Genesis 8:22 NIV).

God tells us that as long as the earth remains, seedtime and harvest shall not cease. Every harvest you desire is in a seed. Only a fool will expect a harvest without first identifying and preparing a seed. The harvest is always a reflection of the nature and quality of the seed.

> *Do not be deceived: God cannot be mocked. A man reaps what he sows* (Galatians 6:7).

There is no better time to sow a challenging seed than a time of famine and economic downturn, just like the world is currently experiencing. Let us examine how Isaiah the prophet relates the seed faith principle to a period of economic hardship.

> *My people will live in peaceful dwelling places, in secure homes, in undisturbed places of rest. Though hail flattens the forest and the city is leveled completely, how blessed you will be, sowing your seed by every stream, and letting your cattle and donkeys range free* (Isaiah 32:18-20).

> *"When anyone came to a heap of twenty measures, there were only ten. When anyone went to a wine vat to draw fifty measures, there were only twenty. I struck all the work of your hands with blight, mildew and hail, yet you did not turn to Me," declares the Lord. "From this day on, from this twenty-fourth day of the ninth month, give careful thought to the day when the foundation of the Lord's temple was laid. Give careful thought: Is there yet any seed left in the barn? Until now, the vine and the fig tree, the pomegranate and the olive tree have not borne fruit. From this day on I will bless you"* (Haggai 2:16-19 NIV).

Isaacs's testimony presents a clear instruction for bail-out.

> *Now there was a famine in the land—besides the earlier famine of Abraham's time—and Isaac went to Abimelech king of the Philistines in Gerar. Isaac planted crops in that*

land and the same year reaped a hundredfold, because the Lord blessed him (Genesis 26:1,12).

The phrase "in that land and the same year" showed that Isaac received a harvest right in the middle of the crisis, not after it. It may cause you some pain and inconvenience, but this is the time to create the harvest you desire through your deliberate faith seed. The Bible says that they who sow in tears shall reap with joy. Sometimes a faith seed will cause you some tears.

The Prayer Key

While God's purpose for the covenant children in the midst of the prevailing global economic challenge is clearly revealed, it will take prevailing in the place of prayer to see its manifestation.

…The effectual fervent prayer of a righteous man availeth much (James 5:16).

In the words of John Wesley, "God can do nothing for humanity unless someone asks Him: It seems God is limited by our prayer life."[1]

Ask and it shall be given you…For every one that asketh receiveth… (Matthew 7:7-8).

Our Lord's injunction for us to ask in order to receive our desires is key to manifesting the will of God in these times of economic meltdown. Even though we have established that it is God's plan for His people to laugh and be in abundance financially irrespective of the current world situation, each of us needs to pray in order to experience its reality.

*Therefore I say unto you, What things soever ye desire, when ye pray, believe that ye receive them and **ye shall have them*** (Mark 11:24).

For those who desire to partake of the promised wealth transfer through these seven years of global financial famine, this is the time to prevail in prayer. Having seen that it is the effectual prayer of the righteous that produces results, the question will be: how can our prayers become effectual?

Endnote

1. Kenneth Hagin quoted John Wesley. See http://www.cfaith.com/index.php?option=com_content&view=article&id=13317:plead-your-case&catid=50:prayer.

9
SIX KEYS TO PRAYING EFFECTUALLY

In this chapter we will be exploring the six keys to praying effectually, which is of vital importance when facing financial, spiritual, relational, and even physical challenges. In detail, we will examine these six keys: don't doubt; give no room for unforgiveness; live righteously; give honor to your spouse; give according to God's will; and pray with expectation.

1. Don't Doubt

> *But let him ask in faith, nothing wavering. For he that wavereth is like a wave of the sea driven with the wind and tossed. For let not that man think that he shall receive anything of the Lord. A double minded man is unstable in all his ways* (James 1:6-8).

To explore the tremendous power that is released when we pray effectually, we will have to learn how to deal with doubt. Doubt is like a lid that places a limit on our petitions. God, in His Word, tells us about the need to come to the place of prayer, believing in results. Prayer shouldn't be a religious exercise, neither should it become a routine; but rather, prayer is a living and active way of gaining unlimited access to divine resources.

You may be wondering, *How do I overcome doubt?* Let's now explore four principles that translate us from doubt to faith.

A. Develop intimacy with God.

> *But we all, with open face beholding as in a glass the glory of the Lord, are changed into the same image from glory to glory even as by the Spirit of the Lord* (2 Corinthians 3:18).

When I married my wife 17 years ago, I had no doubt in my heart that even though we were connected spiritually, we had no physical resemblance. While mine is a round face with two little eyes and a large, distinct nose as though an after thought, Akudo's face, on the other hand, is conspicuously oblong, housing a pointed nose and two distinctively large eyes. We both realized that we did not look alike in any way.

Over the past ten years, however, we have had people mistake her for my younger sister or me for her elder brother; and they claim it is on the basis of our physical resemblance. Initially we had difficulty accepting these remarks. However, we have come to realize that through intimacy, we both now seem to look alike and almost talk alike. Natural things are a reflection of the spiritual; the latter giving rise to the former.

We understand that God is His Word—they are both one.

> *In the beginning was the word, and the word was with God and the word was God* (John 1:1).

We also know that our God is a God of faith. Romans 4:17 declares that He calls the things that be not as though they were. God never doubts His word. When He speaks, He does so with absolute assurance and certainty. He told Jeremiah the prophet that He watches over to see to the performance of every word He has spoken (see Jer. 1:12).

The more time we spend with Him through His written Word, the more intimate we soon become with Him and the more doubt invariably begins to give way to faith in our lives.

God's Word in us gives us perfect understanding of His will and His ways. It is this understanding that eliminates doubt and creates the trust we need in order for our prayers to be effective. Accuracy in prayer is vital for believers to experience the reality of the coming financial increase through these seven years of the global financial meltdown.

B. Listen to the testimonies of others.

In the midst of world economic crises, there are Christians whose businesses have reached an all-time high. There are also those whose eyes have been opened to tremendous opportunities concealed beneath the crises. Listening to the testimonies of such people will help build confidence in the integrity of God's word.

Very often, listening to someone's testimony erases doubt and opens our hearts to the chances that such an experience could be ours also. Sometimes, it actually strengthens a person's resolve to believe God for their own testimony. A typical example is found in Mary's encounter with the angel Gabriel shortly before the Holy Spirit conception (see Luke 1:26-38).

The phrase "be it unto me according to Thy word" in Luke 1:38 was the outcome of Elizabeth's testimony that was shared with Mary by the angel Gabriel. Prior to this point, she had doubted the possibility of conceiving a child by the Holy Ghost. The fact that she was a virgin further strengthened her doubt and compounded the situation. Her doubts, however, were erased when she heard that her barren cousin Elizabeth was six months pregnant at a medically impossible age.

This is what usually happens when we hear testimonies of what God is doing in the lives of other believers. We are able to rise above our doubts and believe Him for our own miracles.

C. Give thanks even when you can't see the result.

One way to overcome doubt and be more effective in prayer is to learn to be thankful not only when we see a miracle, but when nothing seems to happen also.

Thanking God in advance for a miracle is an act of faith. The more we offer thanksgiving in anticipation, the more we actively believe for a manifestation. An attitude of thanksgiving produces peace and assurance even in the midst of the fiercest turmoil. Let's examine how Paul the apostle makes the connection between both of these.

> *Be careful* [worried] *for nothing; but in everything by prayer and supplication* **with thanksgiving** *let your requests be made known unto God. And the peace of God, which passeth all understanding, shall keep your hearts and minds through Christ Jesus* (Philippians 4:6-7).

You will notice that in this passage from Philippians God did not use the phrase "*and* thanksgiving," rather He said, "*with* thanksgiving." What is the significance? It means that each prayer and supplication should be accompanied with thanksgiving. Thanking Him in anticipation puts the ball in His court and in a way commits Him in your situation. This attitude should dominate the period between making a supplication and seeing its manifestation.

In the natural, when a person thanks you in advance for something, it won't be long before you may begin to feel under pressure to do it for them, unless it is not within your capacity. This was the picture our Lord Jesus Christ sort of painted in the parable of the importunate friend.

> *And He said unto them, Which of you shall have a friend, and shall go unto him at midnight, and say unto him, Friend lend me three loaves, for a friend of mine in his journey is come to me and I have nothing to set before him? And he from within shall answer and say, Trouble me not: the door is now shut, and my children are with me in bed; I cannot rise and give thee. I say unto you, Though he will not rise and give him, because he is his friend, yet because of his importunity he will rise and give him as many as he needeth. And I say unto you, ask and it shall be given you…* (Luke 11:5-9).

The word *importune* actually means to press urgently. Even though it wasn't convenient for the householder to respond to his friend's need, he had to do it because of his persistence and pressure. One way to press urgently in prayer is to persistently thank God in advance for your needs. While we cannot put God under pressure to bless us, our persistent thanksgiving, however, can open doors of miracles in our lives.

After we have prayed for a particular need, we are to watch for its manifestation with an attitude of thanksgiving. Let's see how Paul the apostle puts it in Colossians 4:2, "Continue in prayer and watch in the same *with thanksgiving.*"

D. Confess the Word, not the world.

One of the most effective ways of overcoming doubts is never to confess them, but rather to maintain your confession of God's word. Doubt is of the soul, and there is a link between it and your mouth.

> *Whoso keepth his mouth and tongue keepeth his soul from troubles* (Proverbs 21:23).

People's souls are in trouble when they are dominated by doubts, and one sure way to get rid of it is to keep God's word their mouths. The more we speak His Word, the more we believe it. When people have difficulties believing the Word of God, the first thing to check is how much of it they have learned to release through their mouths. The content of people's hearts is directly proportional to the content of their mouths.

In order to get rid of doubt in us, we must flood our hearts with the Word of God; and for His Word to get into our hearts, it must first get into our mouths.

Are we joining everyone else in confessing that our world is in financial crises or are we declaring that there is no better time for increase than now? For how long should we confess it? For as long as it takes to settle it in our hearts that it is done. God, in Job 5:22, affirms that at destruction and famine, His children will laugh. What the world is currently experiencing is likened to famine, and God promises for us to laugh in the midst of it. We should confess that though there is a global economic meltdown, it is our time to laugh.

Now we come to the second of our six keys to effectual praying.

2. Give no Room for Unforgiveness

And when ye stand praying forgive…that your Father also which is in heaven may forgive you your trespasses… (Mark 11:25-26).

One way to have an effective prayer life is to learn how to forgive. This Scripture in Mark reveals that unforgiveness actually pitches us against God. He never takes sides against us; rather we are the ones who sometimes cause this. As long as we are in this world, offenses will come.

*Then said He [Jesus] unto the disciples, It is impossible but that **offenses** will come…* (Luke 17:1).

People will defraud us one way or the other; they will take advantage of us at some point, we will sometimes be cheated, and at other times lies will be told against us. If all of these happened to our Lord Jesus Christ while He physically walked this earth, it shouldn't be strange that they form part of our Christian experience also.

> *It is enough for the disciple that he be as his master, and the servant as his Lord. If they have called the master of the house Beelzebub, how much more shall they call them of his house hold* (Matthew 10:25).

The offenses and troubles we receive form part of our sacrifice of love. Very often those are the rewards we get for showing love to people. However, we must be careful not to allow any of these to create resentment and unforgiveness against those who offend and hurt us.

If we are going to be mighty in prayer, we must pay attention to this truth. The impact of an offense becomes more profound when it is in response to an act of love. People's initial response to love is rejection. I have come to realize that rejection is the pathway to celebration. Until a person is first rejected, defamed, despised, cheated, and offended, they are not likely to rise to the top in God.

The most vital lessons of life are often learned at such times; character also. Many genuine Christians have either been robbed or delayed in experiencing the promise of God in their lives because they have refused to forgive or release someone who has hurt or offended them.

Job's Testimony

> *And the Lord turned the captivity of Job,* **when he prayed for his friends***: also the Lord gave Job twice as much as he had before* (Job 42:10).

Job's testimony presents a unique connection between forgiveness and receiving answers to our prayer. It shows how we can get tremendously blessed if we will dare to forgive those who have deeply wronged us, no matter how justified we may think we are. In the heat of his trial, Job's closest friends had slandered, betrayed, and accused him of suffering for his wrong doings. These were the same ones who had benefited most from his benevolence.

Humanly speaking, Job had every justification to be bitter against them. He opted for the divine option however, knowing that one of the keys to his total restoration and breakthrough was to forgive and pray for those who hurt him. His change didn't come until he did this. God was waiting for him.

This principle is very vital especially in the times we are living in. God has declared that this seven-year period of global financial turmoil, beginning from 2008, will turn out to be the finest hour for the church. Unfortunately, there may be countless numbers of His people who may not fully walk in the reality of this promise because of bitterness and unforgiveness.

I remember a testimony that sister Stella, the wife of my elder brother Martin, shared with me recently. She was called in to pray with a woman who had just been told by doctors in Belgium that in about six months she would die from a cancer-related terminal ailment. This woman had been prayed for by several men and women of God. While speaking with her, the Holy Spirit revealed to Stella that the woman couldn't be healed because she had bitterness and unforgiveness in her heart. When confronted with this truth, the woman broke down in tears. The long and short of this testimony is that she confessed, repented, and got healed. Isn't God wonderful? That woman could have been robbed of health, which is absolutely God's provision in redemption because of unforgiveness.

There are two primary ways that I am constantly learning to deal with bitterness in my heart. First, I settle it that my enemy is not a natural personality but a spirit personality called satan. He and his demons are the ones who instigate human agents against me; therefore they are the ones against whom my anger and resentment are directed, not people.

> *For we wrestle not against flesh and blood but against principalities, against powers, against the rulers of the darkness of this world, against wicked spirits in high places* (Ephesians 6:12).

Second, I determine that no amount of hatred or animosity by any one against me compares with God's love for me, and I will not jeopardize my relationship with Him in trying to react to whatever pain has been inflicted upon me.

> *…For I am persuaded that neither death, nor life, nor angels, nor principalities, nor powers, nor things present, nor things to come, nor height, nor depth, nor any other creature, shall be able to separate us from the love of God which is in Christ Jesus our Lord* (Romans 8:35-39).

The third key to effectual praying is to live righteously:

3. Live Righteously

Once in Christ, a person receives God's own righteousness as a gift. Salvation is God actually imputing and imparting His very life and nature into a person. This happens at the instant when they believe and confess the lordship of Jesus Christ over their lives.

Let's examine two Scriptures in this regard.

> *For if by one man's offense death reigned by one: much more they which receive abundance of grace and of **the gift of righteousness** shall reign in life by one, Jesus Christ* (Romans 5:17).

> *For He* [God] *hath made Him* [Christ] *to be sin for us who knew no sin; that **we might be made the righteousness** of God in Him* (2 Corinthians 5:21).

Having received His righteousness because of Jesus Christ, God expects us to begin to live out the new life that we have received. In other words, we are expected to live righteously. Righteous living is not optional for the believer; it is mandatory. We have received God's righteousness and are empowered by His Spirit to do so. This was John's message in First John 2:29:

> *If ye know that He is righteous, ye know that every one that **doeth righteousness** is born of Him.*

We are expected to do righteousness after we become born again because that is who we are in Christ Jesus. Just as it is taken for granted that a lion should live out its nature, so is righteousness for God's children.

On the contrary, when those who have received God's gift of righteousness fail to begin to live out who they really are and instead start to meddle in sin, it can affect their prayer lives in three fundamental ways.

A. Sin and the human conscience.

> *For if our heart condemn us, God is greater than our heart, and knoweth all things. Beloved, if our heart condemn us not, then have we confidence toward God. And whatsoever we ask* [in prayer], *we receive of Him, **because we keep His commandments and do those things that are pleasing in His sight*** (1 John 3:20-22).

The principle in the Scripture from First John 3 can be summarized in the following order.

- We ought to obey God's commandments and do those things that please Him.
- Obedience creates confidence and a pure conscience toward God.
- By this confidence toward God as a result of obedience, we receive answer to prayer.

Sin, if not repented of, dampers a person's conscience toward God and weakens his or her confidence in prayer. Sin also creates fear in a person; we see two instances in the Bible that clearly present the relationship between them.

The first instance occurs after Adam and Eve disobeyed God and ate the forbidden fruit in the Garden of Eden.

> *And the Lord God called unto Adam, and said unto him Where art thou? And he said I heard Thy voice in the garden, and **I was afraid**…and He* [God] *said…Hast thou eaten of the tree, whereof I commanded thee that thou shouldest not eat?* (Genesis 3:9-11)

What was the cause of Adam's fear? Disobedience, of course. He had just eaten of the tree of the knowledge of good and evil in defiance of God's instruction. This is what happens when a child of God starts to meddle with sin—fear comes in; and at the instance of fear, it is impossible to exercise one's faith in prayer. It is only through repentance and confession that faith is again restored.

We need to understand this principle especially as we pray and believe God to experience the promised financial increase in the midst of the prevailing global economic meltdown. Sin can hinder us in prayer.

The second example of how sin can have a negative impact in our prayer life is found in Genesis 12:1-13.

Abraham's sudden apprehension over his safety stemmed from one fundamental factor: He had disobeyed God in departing from the land of Canaan into Egypt. He obviously was no longer acting in faith; otherwise, he would have been conscious of God's continued presence and His unfailing ability to protect and preserve him. God was with him all the while—even when he walked away from God's will.

This act of disobedience, however, took away the consciousness of His presence from Abraham. This is how sin and disobedience affects a Christian's prayer life. Such a person soon loses consciousness of God's presence in his or her life even though it is still there; the person becomes afraid and ultimately unable to exercise faith in the place of prayer.

B. Sin as a wall of separation

> *Behold, the Lord's hand is not shortened, that it cannot save; neither His ear heavy, that it cannot hear: But your iniquities have separated between you and your God...* (Isaiah 59:1-2).

In this Scripture from Isaiah, sin is pictured as a separating barrier that comes between God and humankind, thereby making it difficult for His blessing to reach us. It also makes it impossible for God to hear a person in prayer. The essence of this study is not to build sin consciousness in us but rather to stimulate our desire for righteous living.

C. Sin as a withholding hand

> *Your iniquities have turned away these things, and your* **sins have withholden good things from you** (Jeremiah 5:25).

Jeremiah, the prophet in this Scripture, presents sin as an invisible hand that withholds good things from reaching a person. God has promised good things for the church; for example, the promised wealth transfer through the current financial shaking is a good thing. However, our attention is being drawn to the fact that if some of us do not deal with sin, disobedience, and certain negative habits in our lives, any of these could constitute the invisible hand that can withhold its manifestation.

Thank God for the blood of Jesus Christ that constantly speaks better things on our behalf (see Heb. 12:24) and cleanses us from all unrighteousness once we confess our wrong doings (see 1 John 1:8-9).

We cannot possibly live in disobedience and at the same time be mighty in prayer. Sin, once recognized, must be dealt with in the place of repentance and confession. We must never justify any wrongdoing, otherwise the enemy can take advantages of us.

I see you realigning yourself with the will of God and taking hold of His promises. *This is your time.*

The fourth key to effective praying is to give honor to your spouse.

4. GIVE HONOR TO YOUR SPOUSE

Like wise, ye husbands, dwell with them according to knowledge, giving honor unto the wife as unto the weaker vessel, and as being heirs together of the grace of life; ***that your prayers be not hindered*** (1 Peter 3:7).

Over the years, I have come to observe that men who dehumanize their wives hardly make substantial progress in life; and even when they do, it is usually short-lived. I couldn't make the connection between the way we relate with our spouses and our effectiveness in prayer, until I got saved and came across the Scripture in First Peter.

Sometimes a person could wonder why, in spite of all they have done—prayed, fasted, sown seed—they do not seem to receive answers to their prayers. The reason could be that they haven't treated their spouses rightly. Even though I may not fully comprehend how this principle works, I have learned to obey it. Simple obedience to the Word of God is the key to walking in the miraculous.

If we are going to be mighty in prayer, we will have to learn to be fair to our spouses. When we dishonor, mistreat, subdue, disrespect, oppress, and generally make life difficult for them, we hinder ourselves in the place of prayer.

Some societies tell us it is weakness on the part of a man to give honor, dignity, and respect to his wife; the Bible on the contrary, tells us it is the wisdom of God. I do not associate closely with men who do not show respect for the opposite sex. The reason is that we ultimately become products of our associations. Paul the apostle, in First Corinthians 15:33, reveals that "…evil communications corrupt good manners."

The fifth key to effective prayers is to ask according to God's will.

5. Ask according to God's will

And this is the confidence that we have in Him, that if we ask anything according to His will He heareth us… (1 John 5:14-15).

God's will is His Word. To be effective in our prayer lives therefore, we must find out what it says concerning any given subject or situation and take that word to Him. This is what prayer is. Let us examine how Hosea the prophet relates this principle to the prayer of repentance and forgiveness for Israel.

> *O Israel, return unto the Lord thy God; for thou hast fallen by thine iniquity.* ***Take with you words, and turn to the Lord...*** (Hosea 14:1-2).

According to Hosea, the only way Israel could be sure of God's forgiveness and restoration was for her to locate His word that guarantees it. They were now to bring those words to Him knowing that God will surely preserve the integrity of His word concerning any situation as well as watch over it to see to its performance.

This principle finds application not only in the area of the prayer of repentance and restoration but also concerning all other aspects of our needs. Has God given us His word concerning the current global shaking? Yes, He has. It is all over the pages of this book. Has He revealed His will concerning it? Yes, He has: His word is His will. What then are we to do when we pray? Take these words one after the other back to Him. God's word is so infallible that He has exalted it above all His name. (See Psalm 138:2.) It is the immutability of His word that makes Him God.

The last important key to praying effectively is to pray with expectation.

6. Pray with Expectation

> *So shall the knowledge of wisdom be unto thy soul: when thou hast found it, then there shall be a reward,* ***and thy expectation shall not be cut off*** (Proverbs 24:14).

Religious praying is no praying. Many of us pray simply because the Bible admonishes us to do so or because we have read a book on prayer. We do not yet see it as an active and living channel through which we can receive the blessings of God. The result is that when we pray, we simply do so for the sake of it; we do not actively expect the things we pray about to come to pass.

Expectation is the womb of manifestation. It should dominate the period between supplication and manifestation. In other words, after we have prayed for a need, we should wait for its manifestation in active expectation. For example, the way you would wait for someone with whom you have a special appointment will certainly be different from your attitude toward a regular visitor to your home.

In the case of the later, you would wake up on the day of the special appointment with expectations. You would probably have selected appropriate dress for the occasion the previous night. As the clock ticks to that crucial moment, your eyes, your ears and your entire focus will be on the door.

Why is it so? Because *you are expecting a knock* on that door. This is the attitude that should characterize our waiting period. God has spoken concerning the ongoing strategic wealth transfer to the church: you may have been praying about it. However, the big question is: *Are you expecting it?*

10
THE LOVE WALK

God's will, as revealed through His Word, is for the church to experience unprecedented financial advancement in the midst of the prevailing global economic adversity. However, in order for us to fully begin to walk in the reality of this promise, we have to learn to *walk in love*—God's kind of love.

When we are not walking in love, we ultimately put limitations both on ourselves and on God in our lives. This can happen in three primary ways: our faith becomes limited; our prayers become ineffective; and we hinder our access to divine secrets.

1. Our Faith Becomes Limited

But without faith it is impossible to please Him… (Hebrews 11:6).

The connection between our faith and our walk of love is very crucial because love affects the most fundamental principle of our relationship with our heavenly Father—our *faith*. Paul the apostle, through the Holy Spirit, reveals this connection in his epistle to the Galatians:

> *For in Jesus Christ neither circumcision availeth any thing, nor uncircumcision; but **faith** which worketh by **love*** (Galatians 5:6).

In this Scripture from Galatians, Paul reveals that faith cannot work without love. If we are going to be people of faith, we must begin by learning to walk in love. Our hopes cannot produce results without faith, and our faith cannot work without love. We need active, productive faith in order to experience the reality of the coming wealth transfer to the Church of Christ through the current world financial turmoil. Such kind of faith, however, is released when we actively start to love people with the God-kind of love.

Faith Versus Love

> *And now abideth faith, hope, charity [love], these three: but the greatest of these is charity [love]* (1 Corinthians 13:13).

Paul the apostle, in emphasizing the indispensability of walking in love for the believer, takes his argument a step further. He affirms that if viewed on a scale, love will be found to outweigh both faith and hope respectively.

> *He that loveth not knoweth not God, for **God is love*** (1 John 4:8).

We understand from the Scripture from First John 4:8 that God is love. If this is truly so, it means we can use the words *love* and *God* interchangeably. For example, rather than say "In the beginning was the word…and the word was *God*," we can also say "In the beginning was the word…and the word was *love*."

If God is love, it simply follows that walking in love will be the same as walking in God, and if we are walking in God, then we are walking in His realm. I have observed over time that people who walk in love often manifest the power and presence of God. This is because they have learned to walk in Him.

When we are not walking in the God-kind of love, we limit our faith, and once our faith is limited, God becomes limited in the various aspects of our lives—whether in our health, finances, ministry, business, or career.

Job's Restoration

Job was previously mentioned regarding forgiveness and how the secret of Job's restoration was that he prayed for his friends—the ones who despised and turned their backs on him. Actions are better appreciated if we take time to know the motivation behind each one. Job was constrained by a principle that is found in a series of statements made by our Lord Jesus Christ in Matthew 5:43-45 (NKJV):

> *You have heard that it was said, "You shall love your neighbor and hate your enemy." But I say to you, **love your enemies, bless those who curse you, do good to those who hate you, and pray for those who spitefully use you and persecute you.***

It was Job's continued love for those who ran him down when they should have been the ones to stand by him in his trials that constrained him to pray for them. He prayed for them because he first loved them. It was an unconditional one; God's kind of love.

Instead of hatred, bitterness, and ill-will toward these ones, he made the hard but wise choice to walk in love. This was the secret of his restoration. To imagine that God did nothing concerning his recovery and restoration until He passed the love test, shows how important and indispensable it is for us to walk in love toward all—whether loveable or not.

As the world struggles under the intense weight of an individualistic and self-centered spirit of darkness, God's people must burst forth as light and begin to shine the unspeakable love of their Lord and Master Jesus Christ. Herein lies the key to experiencing God's promise of strategic wealth transfer to the church through the ongoing global financial and economic turmoil. The more we love, the more we will have.

2. Our Prayers Become Ineffective

And whatsoever we ask, we receive of Him, because we keep His commandments, and do those things that are pleasing in His sight. And this is His commandment; that we should believe on the name of His Son Jesus Christ, and **love one another***, as He gave us commandment* (1 John 3:22-23).

We established earlier, from Galatians 5:6, that faith works by love. In other words, our faith can only be active and productive if we walk in love toward one another. From the Scripture in First John 3 also, we see that for us to receive His commandment for us to love one another walking in love is a command and not an option. Putting Galatians 5:6 together with First John 3:22-23, it follows that if our faith needs our love to work, and our prayers need our faith to produce results, that puts love in a critical position. Without love there can be no faith, and without faith we cannot receive answers to our prayers.

When we walk in hatred and bitterness toward people, we short-change ourselves in the blessings of God. Research has even linked a number of health conditions, like cancer and arthritis, to harboring bitterness and hatred.

3. We Hinder Our Access to Divine Secrets

For this cause I bow my knees unto the Father of our Lord Jesus Christ, of whom the whole family in heaven and earth is named, that He would grant you, according to the riches of His glory, to be strengthened with might by His spirit in the inner man. That Christ may dwell in your heart by faith; that ye being rooted and grounded in love, may be able to comprehend with all saints what is the breadth, and length, and depth, and height... (Ephesians 3:14-19).

The breath, length, depth, and height in the Scripture represents insight and revelation into the secret things of God. Access to such privileged information is only for those who are rooted and grounded in their love walk.

Insight into divine secrets is what distinguishes one Christian from another. Your height in life is a function of your insight, and the latter is a function of love. Hatred, bitterness, and ill-will toward people, on the other hand, can short-circuit a person's access to such divine wisdom, and ultimately bring them to a place of spiritual dryness.

Your degree of revelation will determine your level of ascension and acceleration. You ascend in life on the basis of what is revealed to you. Rather than spend your whole time fasting and praying for wisdom and revelation, you should simply grow in your love walk. This is what the Bible says, and it's as simple as that.

The more we love others unconditionally, the more insight we have into the wisdom of God. In this season of economic hardship, it is the operation of this wisdom in believers that will make a difference—whether in their business career or ministry.

The reason why some people may not fast long days or make lengthy prayers, and yet continue to abound in revelation and wisdom is because they have learned not to permit hatred, bitterness, jealousy, ill-will, and unforgiveness, but rather to abound in love both toward those who love them as well as those who hate them.

A person is filled with the fullness of God according to their degree of revelation knowledge of Him, and this knowledge is a function of love.

> *And to know the love of Christ, which passeth knowledge that ye might be filled with all the fullness of God* (Ephesians 3:19).

Is it possible for a Christian to be filled with all the fullness of God? Absolutely yes. How can this happen? By knowing the love of Christ. The essence of this knowledge of the love of Christ is so that we might walk in it as well as show it forth to others. The more we do this, the more we are filled with all the fullness of God; and the more we are filled with all His fullness, the more unlimited we become. God wants us to live life beyond limits.

A person who is filled with all the fullness of God cannot be affected by the elements of this world—whether economic, social, or political. Such a person lives an unlimited life. This is the calling of the church of Christ. Our lives should not and must not be defined by the things happening around us. We are Heaven's ambassadors here in this earth realm, "Now then we are ambassadors for Christ…" (2 Cor. 5:20).

The economic, social, and political environment of this world does not define the way we live. It is Heaven's environment that regulates and determines how we live on this earth's environment; that's why even in the midst of the prevailing global financial meltdown, God's people can and should shout their way through all of it.

*For our conversation is in **heaven**...* (Philippians 3:10).

The Greek word for conversation in the Philippians 3 context is *politeuma*, which means government and citizenship. What does a government do? It protects and provides for its citizens, while also ensuring the appropriate economic, social, and political climate.

If our government is in Heaven, then we can boldly expect Heaven to protect and provide for our every need here, irrespective of the current harsh global financial situation. This is God's message to the church.

Those who choose to walk in love toward others are the ones who will have the privilege of comprehending the depth, height, breadth, and length of His work in the seasons in which we currently live. They are the ones to whom He will make known His plan and purpose for the church and the world in these times of crises.

Hatred and bitterness will keep a person in darkness. It is love that will break up the seals and make known the mysteries of His will. It is love that will remove the veils of ignorance. It was love that tore the veil in two in the Most Holy Place. It is love that will cause our ears to begin to hear God's voice in the midst of this shaking.

11
A Message to the World

I believe that God gave me the revelation about the seven-year worldwide crisis because He knew I would share it with His children and all who would listen. I pray this book and the wisdom God reveals through it will reach around the world and will help all who read it to know that He is in control—and that He loves each person uniquely and completely.

It is so important for all believers to share with the world that He is the only God who can bring peace and hope in the midst of any turmoil—financial, emotional, physical, relational, and spiritual. While wars rage worldwide between nations and more personal wars rage within, God, through the sacrifice of Jesus Christ and with the help of the Holy Spirit brings inner strength and joy that is beyond any human understanding.

This is the message we must take to the world. Start with yourself—believe it firmly and proclaim it boldly. Then by example share your zeal with your family, neighbors, coworkers, community, and beyond.

It is also important to understand who the people of this world are. Based on the following Scripture verse, I believe there are basically three groups of people in existence today: the Jews; the Gentiles; and the Church of God.

> *Give none offense, neither to the **Jews**, nor to the **Gentiles**, nor to the **Church of God*** (1 Corinthians 10:32).

I will expand on these three groups to clearly define each—giving you the information you need to fully understand God's desire in these trying times.

The Seed of Abraham

The Jews and the Church of God constitute the seed of Abraham, both representing two nations that are linked to God by covenant. While the Jews represent a physical and geographical nation in covenant with Him, the Church represents a spiritual one. Paul the apostle explains this connection in his epistle to the Romans.

> *For the promise, that he* [Abraham] *should be the heir of the world, was not to Abraham, or his **seed** through the law, but* [to his seed] *through the righteousness of faith* (Romans 4:13).

This Scripture clearly reveals that Abraham has two seeds: first, the Jews who are his seed through the law; and second, the Church of God who are his seed through the righteousness of faith. Both are in a covenant relationship with God; the former through the Abrahamic covenant and the latter through the Messianic covenant.

Many have argued that God's covenant with the Jews through Abraham has been nullified by the new covenant in the blood of Jesus Christ. The truth is this: while the latter is a better covenant established upon better promises, the former is still in His heart.

God is forever mindful of His covenant. Psalms 105, 106, and 111 support both positions respectively.

> *The covenant which He made with Abraham, and His oath to Isaac* (Psalm 105:9 NKJV).

> *And for their sake He remembered His covenant, and relented according to the multitude of His mercies* (Psalm 106:45 NKJV).

> *He has given food to those who fear Him; He will ever be mindful of His covenant* (Psalm 111:5 NKJV).

THE POSITION OF THE CHURCH

"By so much was Jesus made a surety of a better testament" (Heb. 7:22). Another word for testament as seen in this Scripture is *covenant*. "But now hath He [Jesus] obtained a more excellent ministry, by how much also He is the mediator of a better covenant, which was established upon better promises" (Heb. 8:6).

THE POSITION OF THE JEWS

> *And so all Israel shall be saved: as it is written, There shall come out of Zion the Deliverer, and shall turn away ungodliness from Jacob. For this is My covenant unto them, when I shall take away their sins. As concerning the gospel they [the Jews] are enemies for your sakes: but as touching the election,* **they are beloved for the father's sakes** (Romans 11:26-28).

The phrase "they are beloved for the father's sakes" reveals that Israel still has a privileged place in the heart of God, as a result of His covenant with the fathers, prominent among whom was

Abraham. Israel's calling is still in place. This was the picture Paul the apostle tried to convey in Romans 11:29-31:

> *For the gifts and calling of God are without repentance. For as ye* [Gentiles] *in times past have not believed God, Yet have now obtained mercy, through their unbelief: Even so have these* [Jews] *also now not believed that through your mercy they also may obtain mercy.*

THE GENTILE WORLD

Two groups are represented in the Gentile world: 1) any one who is neither a Jew nor belongs to the Body of Christ, and 2) secular governments. Generally speaking, a person is either an Israelite, a Christian, or a Gentile.

The question this chapter addresses is: *Can the Gentile world experience God's blessing in the midst of the global economic shaking?*

The answer is yes.

The key to the blessing is found in one of the most profound pronouncements God made to Abraham. An individual or secular government that will recognize, accept, and apply this principle will experience the supernatural blessings of God even in the midst of the current global financial crises. The pronouncement is found in Genesis 12:1-3:

> *Now the Lord had said unto Abram, Get thee out of thy country, and from thy kindred, and from thy father's house...and I will bless them that bless thee....*

The pronouncement may be so inconspicuous but yet so profound. It creates a rare and unusual access to the blessings of God for those who may not be in a covenant relationship with Him. However, it is only through the shed blood of Jesus Christ that a person's eternal destiny can be secured. After all, what does it profit a person to gain the whole world and lose his soul? (See Matthew 16:26.)

What Then Is the Message?

If an individual—irrespective of race, tribe, or secular government, whether at the national, provincial, state, or local government level—will dare to key into this principle of blessing and favoring the cause of both the Jewish people and the Church of Christ, they will experience the blessings of the Lord even in the midst of these crises.

The Scriptures clearly affirm categorically that prosperity will be the experience of those who love God's covenant people, whether the Jews or the Church irrespective of prevailing circumstances.

> *Pray for the peace of Jerusalem: they* [irrespective of race] *shall prosper* [irrespective of circumstances] *that love thee* (Psalm 122:6).

The Bible talks about two Jerusalems: a physical one that is associated with the Jewish people, and a spiritual one associated with the Church of Christ.

> *For this Agar is mount Sinai in Arabia, and answereth to Jerusalem which now is…But Jerusalem which is above is free which is the mother of us all* (Galatians 4:25-26).

Anyone who will love the Jews and Christians, whether they are individuals or governments, will enjoy prosperity even in the midst of the current global financial challenge. Unfortunately, today many nations worldwide seem to have turned their backs on the Jewish nation of Israel. Some leaders have even called for the Jews to be "wiped off the face of the earth."[1] We can't allow this to happen, for believers know that the Jews are God's chosen people—those who pray for the peace of both Jerusalems and who love God will prosper.

A Message to Secular Governments

Wise governments more than ever before should understand that this is the season to begin to legislate laws and formulate policies that will favor and support Israel and Christians. Such laws or policies could be to create an atmosphere that will secure and foster the stability of the Jewish people wherever they are, as well as legislated, periodic financial support to the church for the work of the gospel. As foolish as this may sound, experience has shown that governments who have dared to do this have prospered and attained greater economic stability than the rest.

A Message to Gentile Individuals

This same principle is true for persons who, irrespective of where they come from, choose to love and support God's covenant people.

Let's examine two examples in the Bible regarding this principle.

"And Laban said unto him [Jacob], I pray thee, if I have found favor in thine eyes, tarry: for I have learned by experience that *the Lord hath blessed me for thy sake*" (Gen. 30:27). Laban was a Gentile, yet God blessed him because he blessed Jacob.

"…And it came to pass from the time that he [Potiphar] had made him [Joseph] overseer in his house, and over all that he had, that *the Lord blessed the Egyptian's house for Joseph's sake…*" (Gen. 39:3-5). Because Potiphar blessed Joseph by promoting him in his job, God in turn blessed Potiphar and his entire household greatly.

Leaders and governments that oppress God's people, whether Jews or Christians, and formulate policies that tend to hinder the work of the gospel ultimately slow down their prosperity.

You can inspire and motivate Gentile people you come in contact with by being an example of God's love and righteousness. Dare to do the right thing when you have choices to make. Step out into the water of honesty and integrity and refresh yourself, which will refresh those around you as well. Climb over the obstacles that stand in your way of becoming all that God intended you to be—a bright beacon of light in this darkened world.

It is my sincere desire during this global storm that you will reach out to God and receive the blessings and treasures He has stored up especially for you. Take advantage of His love for you—realize that He is your only Hope in the storms that you are facing today or will ever face in all your tomorrows.

Endnote

1. Ewen MacAskill, Chris McGreal, "Israel should be wiped off map, says Iran's President," The Guardian, October 27, 2005, http://www.guardian.co.uk/world/2005/oct/27/israel.iran; accessed April 18, 2011.

He who has an ear, let him hear
what the Spirit says to the churches…

(Revelation 2:7 NKJV).

About the Author

Ugo Ikpeazu met Christ Jesus in August 1993. From 1996, he served as associate pastor of the Redeemed Christian Church of God's El-Shaddai Worship Center in Surulere, Lagos, Nigeria. Four years later, he relocated his family to Abuja, Nigeria, by divine instruction, where he cofounded the Everlasting Arms Parish of the Redeemed Christian Church of God.

In October 2002, in response to the voice of the Holy Spirit, he founded The Triumphant Ministry. The ministry has established missions within and outside Nigeria. For more information about The Triumphant Ministry, visit the church website at www.thetriumphantministry.com.

Pastor Ugo also serves as the president and founder of the International School of Ministry (ISM), the Climate and Environmental Rescue (CARE) Initiative, and the Royal Bible Institute, which has centers in Nigeria, South Africa, and Uganda.

Pastor Ikpeazu lives in Abuja with his wife, Dr. Akudo Ikpeazu, a public health practitioner, and their three boys: Ugo, Ifeanyi, and Koseku.

CONTACT THE AUTHOR

To contact pastor Ugo Ikpeazu, please e-mail him at:
pastorugo@ttmigospel.info
Or visit his website at:
www.ttmigospel.info

A new, exciting title from
DESTINY IMAGE™ EUROPE

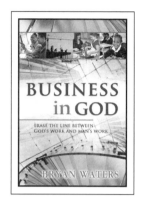

BUSINESS IN GOD
Erase the line between God's work and man's work

by Bryan Waters

- What is my destiny in Christ?
- What has God called me to be and do—in and for His Kingdom?
- What is His plan for my life?
- How can I draw and live closer to God?

If' you've ever asked yourself any of these questions, the answer is waiting for you!

Business in God discusses in a refreshingly simple way that even though you may be in a career or involved in daily activities that seem "non-spiritual," you can still be, and should be, on course to fulfill your God-given destiny.

Author and entrepreneur Bryan Waters shares how you can "prosper in all things" and how to apply the revelation to your daily life in practical ways.

ISBN: 978-88-96727-24-9

Order now from Destiny Image Europe
Telephone: +39 085 4716623 +39 085 8670146
Email: orders@eurodestinyimage.com
Internet: www.eurodestinyimage.com

Additional copies of this book and other book titles from DESTINY IMAGE™ EUROPE are available at your local bookstore.

We are adding new titles every month!

To view our complete catalog online, visit us at:
www.eurodestinyimage.com

Send a request for a catalog to:

Via della Scafa, 29/14
65013 Città Sant'Angelo (Pe), ITALY
Tel. +39 085 4716623 • +39 085 8670146
Fax +39 085 9090113
info@eurodestinyimage.com

"Changing the world, one book at a time."

Are you an author?

Do you have a "today" God-given message?

CONTACT US

We will be happy to review your manuscript for the possibility of publication:

publisher@eurodestinyimage.com
http://www.eurodestinyimage.com/pages/AuthorsAppForm.htm